*To Vivi & Paul,
Thanks for all the memories we made in the Great North Woods.*

9/8/2012

A Protestant Discovers Mary

A Place for Mary in Our Faith and Worship

By Gary R. Shiplett

Gary R. Shiplett

PublishAmerica
Baltimore

© 2009 by Gary R. Shiplett.
All rights reserved. No part of this book may be reproduced, stored in a retrieval system or transmitted in any form or by any means without the prior written permission of the publishers, except by a reviewer who may quote brief passages in a review to be printed in a newspaper, magazine or journal.

First printing

PublishAmerica has allowed this work to remain exactly as the author intended, verbatim, without editorial input.

ISBN: 978-1-4489-9411-3
PUBLISHED BY PUBLISHAMERICA, LLLP
www.publishamerica.com
Baltimore

Printed in the United States of America

To my sister Nancy Lee (Shiplett) Anderson, who has encouraged me to publish my work on Mary for a number of years and considered this her favorite from among all that I have written.

Contents

Introduction 7
Describes the author's own discovery of Mary as a Christian model and calls for a recognition of Mary among Protestant Christians.
A Note on Study Groups 10

Part One: Discovering Mary in the Biblical Text and in the Tradition
CHAPTER 1:
MARY: THE DREAM AND THE REALITY 15
Study Aids 24
Challenges both Protestant and Catholic Christians to take a fresh look at Mary the Mother of Jesus as she is set forth in the New Testament.

CHAPTER 2:
MARY: A MODEL FOR ALL CHRISTIANS 26
Study Aids 37
Summarizes how both the Protestant Reformers and the Catholic Church have portrayed Mary. It holds up Mary in her devotion to God's will as a model for all Christians.

CHAPTER 3: "HAIL MARY, FULL OF GRACE" 39
Study Aids 51
Portrays the divine Motherhood of Mary as set forth in the creeds, the Catholic Church's Tradition, and in Scripture.

CHAPTER 4: MARY, THE ONE FAVORED BY GOD 53
Study Aids 60
Retells the story of how Mary was chosen and what it means to be chosen by God. Compares Mary's consecration to the Wesleyan Covenant Prayer.

CHAPTER 5: 'WHY DID THIS HAPPEN TO ME?' 62
Study Aids 70
> *Describes Mary's visit to Elizabeth and discusses the meaning of God's summons to obedience even when it involves suffering.*

CHAPTER 6: MARY'S SONG: THE MAGNIFICAT 72
Study Aids 80
> *Explores the meaning of this revolutionary song of Mary which embodies God's 'preferential option' for the poor and oppressed.*

CHAPTER 7: THE OBEDIENCE OF JOSEPH 82
Study Aids 91
> *Examines Mary's summons to bear God's Son from the view-point of Joseph and the dangers that threatened Mary. Gives a fresh appreciation for the role and character of Joseph.*

CHAPTER 8:
MARY IN THE LIFE AND MINISTRY OF JESUS 93
Study Aids 104
> *Examines how Mary is portrayed outside the nativity narratives in the four Gospels and in the Book of Acts.*

CHAPTER 9: RELATIONSHIPS IN
THE AGE OF EVE AND THE AGE OF MARY 107
Study Aids 117
> *Uses the ancient hermeneutical principle of Eve/Mary to examine and interpret biblical passages dealing with relationships between male and female. The Age of Mary is contrasted with the Age of Eve. It challenges those passages that reflect the Age of Eve with its subordination of woman as man's 'helpmate' in light of the new Age of Mary in which woman is now a partner with God in the salvation of the world.*

CHAPTER 10: TITLES FOR MARY 119
Study Aids 132
> *A list of some of the most common and some of the most important titles for Mary. Two of the most ancient, the most controversial, and, among Protestant Christians, the most misunderstood titles for Mary are here discussed. These are "Mother of God," and "Theotokos."*

CHAPTER 11: A WAY FORWARD 135
Study Aids 143
> *Protestants are asked to be faithful to their own tradition when they encounter Mary in the biblical text. The reader is encouraged to find a way forward in recovering Mary in our faith and worship. Two lists are given suggesting small steps that can move Protestant readers forward. The first list is for both laity and clergy, while the second list is primarily for pastors.*

Part Two: Recovering Mary in Our Worship
CHAPTER 12: MARY IN OUR LITURGY 149
> *Liturgical resources including calls to worship and dismissals that incorporate Mary into our congregational worship.*

CHAPTER 13: MARY, THE MOTHER OF JESUS 156
> *A Christmas program honoring Mary with narrative and carols*

CHAPTER 14: Born In Bethlehem: A Pilgrimage 162
> *Another Christmas program honoring Mary with narrative and carols*

CONCLUSION 171
> *Challenges both Protestant pastors and laity to set aside all the obstacles that hinder them from discovering Mary in the text of Scripture and in the Tradition of the Church.*

ENDNOTES 175
SCRIPTURE INDEX 178
READING LIST 183

Introduction

This little book is a personal invitation from me to you. It is an invitation to visit some very familiar texts of scripture, texts that every Sunday school child soon learns. I want you to visit these texts with me. There is only one request I make of you as we begin our journey together. Please travel lightly with me. Do not take any unnecessary baggage with you on the trip. If you stand in the Protestant tradition, which prides itself in embracing scripture as its primary authority, then please leave behind all the anti-Catholic biases and anti-Mary prejudices that you have inherited. For these will stand in the way of the text and subvert it. Protestants have been exposed to a number of practices among our Catholic sisters and brothers, which seem quite confusing to us. This confusion is only exacerbated by a number of assumptions we make about Marion devotion. As we take this journey together, you will find that a number of these assumptions are not well informed.

Perhaps one of the most common assumptions held by many Protestants who are uniformed about the Catholic practice of Marian devotion is based on the confusion of veneration with worship. These persons assume Catholic Christians are worshiping Mary. Of course, they are not. They venerate Mary;

they do not worship her. Such assumptions and biases can hinder us from moving through the text of scripture to meet a very remarkable Christian. If we are to coax her to step out of the text and into the realm of flesh and blood, we must allow the text in all of its pristine freshness and all its life-giving power to come alive for us. If we allow ourselves to stand before the text of scripture unencumbered by the centuries old assumptions, suspicions and divisions, if we have ears to hear and eyes to see along with an open heart, I promise you startling discoveries.

If you stand in the Catholic tradition, which prides itself in embracing our most ancient faith embodied in Tradition and Scripture, then please keep both eyes open on our journey. Keep an eye on the sacred Tradition of the Church and an eye on the sacred Tradition of the biblical text, as Vatican II has taught Catholics to do. For Tradition and Text can enrich and illuminate each other. Those standing in the Catholic tradition have not always enjoyed the full benefits of enriching their Marian devotion with a serious and honest struggling with the meaning of the biblical texts about Mary. The Second Vatican Council,[1] along with Pope Paul VI[2] and Pope John Paul II[3] mark a helpful correction to that deficiency. On this journey which I invite you to take with me, you will need to become a time traveler going back in time to rediscover the Mary of the Bible who helped give rise to the Mary of the Church's Tradition. This, I promise you, will not diminish your love and veneration of the Virgin Mary. It can only deepen it, as many post-Vatican II Catholics and scholars have shown. The Mary you will first meet stepping out of the text of scripture may seem less like a "queen of heaven" and more like a frightened young Jewish girl of thirteen or fourteen years of age. For the Mary we first encounter in the Bible is such a young woman who has just been told that she has been chosen and blessed above all other women to become the Mother of our Lord Jesus Christ.

A PROTESTANT DISCOVERS MARY

Therefore, whether your religious background is Catholic or Protestant, please join me on this very special journey. We will visit a number of different events and times in the life of Mary. Of course, we will visit her in the hour of her Visitation, when the angel Gabriel came to announce Mary's special calling and destiny. We will journey with her to visit Mary's relative Elizabeth who also had been visited by the angel. We will meet Mary in the uncertain moments when it was not yet clear whether Joseph would believe her or abandon her. Then we will watch with Mary and Joseph in the darkness and loneliness of that stable cave in Bethlehem when the dream and the reality clashed with all the thunder of life and death. Afterwards, we will meet Mary from time to time as she appears during the life and ministry of Jesus. We will also see her at the cross and later in the Upper Room praying with the apostles in Jerusalem following the resurrection of our Lord Jesus. We will also examine how Mary appears in the Tradition of the Church and how she was considered by the Protestant Reformers. We will examine how Age of Eve/Age of Mary can be used as a hermeneutical principle to interpret some of the difficult and conflicting biblical texts dealing with subjection and submission of women.

Upon the completion of our journey, none of us may ever be quite the same again. For we will have encountered a most unique and special person associated with our Christian faith. She will be able to teach us much, if we are teachable. She will be able to guide us into the depths of faith, if we will allow ourselves to be so guided. She will challenge any notion we may have about "cheap grace," if grace is important to us. Yes, Mary has much to offer us, if we are prepared to meet her as our friend, our sister, our companion, our teacher, our model, and our Mother in the faith.

Dr. Gary R. Shiplett
Advent

A Note on Study Groups

At the end of each chapter, you will find a series of questions, along with suggestions, that may be used as study aids to reflect on each chapter. I encourage pastors and Christian Educators to provide opportunities for the laity to meet as a study group to work through this book together. The study aids could them be used as discussion questions guided by a leader. Such discussion is not "group think" but rather "group learning," by helping one another deal thoughtfully and personally with the material in each chapter. The atmosphere for such an adult study group needs to be open, supportive, and allow participants to express freely their questions, concerns and doubts in a climate that is free of judgmental behaviors. The role of the group leader is not to provide the "correct" answers but rather to guide the work of the discussion group by facilitating member participation with responsive and supportive leadership, raising questions, helping summarize, and "gate keeping" to help participants who may be less assertive to contribute to the discussion. The discussion leader, then, is more of a *process* person than an expert on the subject matter.

The use of this book as a resource for adult study groups may be structured in a variety of ways. For a four week Advent study, those chapters dealing with the annunciation and birth may be used (e.g. chapters 1-4). For a six week Lenten study, six chapters representing the book may be selected (e.g. chapter 1-5, and 8). A Lenten study should include "Mary in the Life and Ministry of Jesus (Chapter 8), because it deals with Mary at the cross. Of course, in ongoing or long term study groups the book may be studied chapter by chapter through Part I, chapters one through eleven. Part II, with its examples of Mary in common worship, does not need to be discussed. The worship examples, however, may be a helpful addition to the various sessions of the study.

The study aids are only suggestions and aids. It also important to allow time for questions raised by members of the study group. Generally, at least one and a half hours is needed in order to allow adequate time for discussion of each chapter.

PART I

DISCOVERING MARY

*In the Biblical Text
and In the Tradition*

CHAPTER 1
MARY: THE DREAM AND THE REALITY

"Blessed is she who believed..." (Luke 1:45)

Carlo Carretto, an author and monk in the order of the Little Brothers of Jesus, tells a moving story of his own rediscovery of Mary, the mother of Jesus. At first, he reports, his relationship with Mary was somewhat marred by what he called "the romanticism of the type of Marian devotion that was all the rage before the Vatican Council and which gradually became empty of meaning."[4] Such an exalted view of Mary as "a queen to end all queens" had little to say to anguished people struggling in a wilderness of faith. Then it began to happen. While a monk living in the desert, Carlo earned his bread working as a meteorologist. At times, he would stay with an ancient tent-dwelling people in their encampments. Quite by chance, he discovered that a girl in the camp where he was staying was betrothed to a boy in another camp, but she had not yet gone to live with him because she was too young. This, of course, is reminiscent of the gospel account of the betrothal of Mary and Joseph.

Two years later, Carlo again visited that same encampment. He casually inquired whether the marriage had yet taken place. His inquiry was met with a look of embarrassment, followed by an awkward silence. Carlo let the subject drop, for fear of offending his host. However later
that evening when he went to draw water outside the camp, Carlo asked one of the tribal chief's servants what lay behind the awkward silence that met his inquiry. The servant looked cautiously around. Then he made a sign passing his hand under his chin in a gesture characteristic of the Arabs when they want to convey that some one has had his or her throat cut. "Why?" asked Carlo. Before the wedding, the servant reported, it was discovered that the girl was pregnant, and the honor of the betrayed family required this sacrifice. The girl had been killed because she had become pregnant by a man other than her betrothed husband. That evening worshiping beneath the Sahara sky, Carlo Carretto read again the familiar account of the conception of Jesus recorded in the gospel. He writes, "I remember vividly how it was on that evening. I felt that Mary was very close, squatting on the sand, small, weak, defenseless, with her large belly, unable to lean forward, silent."[5] As he put out the candle, Carlo imagined, while sitting there in the dark beneath the star filled desert sky, how the eyes of the people of Nazareth must have pierced the girl-mother while they accused Mary: "What have you done to have this child, you awful wretch, you slut!"

That evening, Carlo reports, he felt for the first time that he was getting close to the real mystery of Mary. For the first time, he saw her not as a static statue on an altar, robed as the 'queen of heaven,' but as a "sister there beside him, seated on the sand of the world, her sandals threadbare like his and with exhaustion in her heart." It was that evening on the sand, reports Carlo, that he decided to choose Mary as his instructor in the faith. Mary had become a companion on the pilgrimage, a teacher in the faith. Those nurtured in Catholic devotion need to liberate Mary from a lifeless place on church altars to a vital place on the sands of the world, to discover Mary as a woman, a creature, a sister, a teacher, a disciple. Those of us nurtured in Protestant devotion need to liberate Mary from the dusty attic of our own neglect, covered with the cobwebs of an inherited anti-Catholic bias against all things Catholic. Only then can we discover Mary as a woman, a sister, a teacher, a disciple, a model for all Christians. Only then can we discover Mary in the fullness of both her humanity and her faith. Only then can she occupy her rightful place in the Christian tradition, neither as an Italian Madonna nor as a queen of heaven but as a first century peasant Jewish woman who was chosen by God to be the Mother of Jesus, the Messiah. Mary can become our companion on the journey, our teacher in the faith.

Hail Mary, full of grace,
the Lord is with thee;
Blessed art thou among women,
and blessed is the fruit of thy womb, Jesus.

We praise Mary the Mother of our Lord, for as Luke declares, "Blessed is she who believed..." Truly God her savior had regarded the low estate of God's handmaiden. Mary was swept-up, through God's summons and her own obedience, into the dream of God for the reordering of all of life, for the salvation of God's creation. Yet poor, tender, innocent Mary! In her body, the dream must take flesh. She is asked to lend her body to what may only be a dream, with no reality. Was the visit of the angel only a dream? Was Mary, while deep in prayer, so overwhelmed with God that she confused dream and reality? To believe that God would become a human being is the greatest possible dream for us. Yet can God and human be so united? Can heaven and earth become one?

Poor Mary! As hard as it was to believe that a young virgin could bear a child, it soon became quite apparent that a child was growing inside her young body. Mary was betrothed to Joseph and, as the Bible so gently puts it, had not known a man. Yet this reality to the dream would become embarrassingly even shamefully true. Yes, a child was soon growing inside her womb. It would no longer take a shred of faith to believe that! Her abdomen was soon swelling with the gift of new life. However, to believe that the baby growing in her womb was the "Son of the Most High," that was perhaps more dream than anything. To conceive the Son of God in her flesh was an easy thing, but to conceive him in faith was considerably more demanding. At the announcement of the angel, Mary was troubled over the thought that she could conceive a child. "And Mary said to the angel, 'How shall this be, since I have no husband?'" (Luke 1:34). Yet from that moment on, the thing that would trouble Mary for the rest of her life, from Bethlehem to Golgotha, was this: "Who is my son? And for what great purpose of God was he born? Was it only a dream, the visitation and the words which the angel had spoken?"

"*...and the Lord God will give to him the throne of his father David, and he will reign over the house of Jacob for ever, and of his kingdom there will be no end." (Luke 1:32-33)*

The throne of King David represented for Mary, as it did for every faithful Jew, the dream of the golden age of Israel. It was King David who had captured Jerusalem and made it both the seat of government and the spiritual center of Israel. It was his dream to build a great temple in Jerusalem to house the Ark of the Covenant of God. That Ark was the most sacred symbol of Israel's faith, since it contained the two stones inscribed with the Ten Commandments of Moses. Out of Israel's dreams associated with the reign of their great king, there emerged the belief that God's 'Anointed One,' called Messiah, would one day restore the fortunes of Israel. Messiah would bring to fulfillment the promises of God embodied in Israel's sacred history. Now the salvation of God's people was to be realized in Mary's son. Could this be true? Mary wanted to believe the dream.

In Bethlehem where Mary's son would be born, the dream became a hard dream. Poor Mary had made the long journey by foot and by donkey down the Jordan Valley from the Galilee where she lived in Nazareth. Then her journey with Joseph took them past the Holy City of Jerusalem south about five more miles to Bethlehem. Although the journey was hardly safe for Mary, coming as it did near the end of her pregnancy, yet it brought a secret thrill to her soul. "Just think, Joseph," Mary said as they passed along in the Kidron Valley between the Mount of Olives to their left and Mount Zion to their right where God's holy Temple stood high above them. "Just maybe my son will be born while we are in Bethlehem. How wonderful it would be that God's Messiah should be born in David's city. A thousand years ago in Bethlehem, David was born. Do you think, Joseph, that maybe God is somehow making it possible for this promised child to be born also in David's city?"

Joseph did not answer. It was not so easy for him to share Mary's dream. His thoughts were already pondering where the two of them would find shelter for the night. Joseph was also from the house of David; he had many relatives in Bethlehem. Surely, someone of them would provide a little comfort for them during their stay in Bethlehem. After all, Mary was near her time for the birth of her son. It would not be good to stay at the local inn. Such places were more for caravans and merchants than for family folks, Joseph reasoned as he picked his way among the broken stone of the valley. We do not know why Joseph was unable to arrange for

Mary and him to stay with relatives while in Bethlehem. It is hard to put a positive construction upon it. With his relatives would be the obvious place to stay. Yet turned away, for whatever reason, the bone-weary couple turned to the local inn as a last resort. However, even there Mary and Joseph were turned away. Appealing to the innkeeper in desperation, they were allowed to take shelter with their little donkey in a nearby stable, which was nothing more than a dark limestone cave with a gate across the front.

Yes, as the youthful Mary tried to find a comfortable position on the floor of the cave with only some straw to smooth out the lumps, the dream became very hard indeed. Somehow, this is not at all the way she had pictured the divine motherhood. Surely the birth of God's Messiah deserved something more. Lying there in the darkness of that cave with exhaustion both in her heart as well as her body, Mary must have wept. No doubt, she wept very softly so as not to upset Joseph. Joseph tried to comfort her, but he had the beast to attend to and water to fetch. How frightened Mary must have been. The visit of the angel now seemed like a fantasy and hardly a dream at all.

During that bitter night of loneliness and hardship, Mary gave birth to her first-born and swaddled him in wrapping cloths and laid him on the hay in the stable manger. "What a miserable beginning for one whom the angel had called holy, the Son of God," she murmured in her heart. The local midwife had been a great help. Mary's son was healthy. Bless God! When nearby shepherds suddenly appeared telling tall tales of angels and a savior's birth, Mary was refreshed. She kept all these things and pondered them in her heart. The dream was still alive and now was becoming real. As difficult as life and birth and rest can be in a stable cave, God was with them. God had not forsaken them. The message of the angel was taking form in human life. Surely, Mary's son must be special indeed.

A PROTESTANT DISCOVERS MARY

Sometime later, by which time the holy family had found housing in Bethlehem, three Wise Men from the East came to their door asking about a newborn who was to be "King of the Jews." Mary wanted to declare that of course they were seeking her son, whom the angel had said would receive the throne of his father David. Yet in her modesty, she said nothing. After all, Joseph spoke to strangers. He represented the family to the outside world. Would Joseph tell of the dream that he had nearly a year ago in which an angel had spoken to him? He was uncomfortable to speak of it, especially to strangers.

However, it was the Wise Men who spoke first. They told of strange things in which their celestial gazing had led them to Israel, while the teaching of the prophet Micah led them to Bethlehem. When the Wise Men had arrived in Jerusalem inquiring about the birth of the "King of the Jews," King Herod was troubled. After all, King Herod was near the end of his reign and was concerned about his successor. Surely, he was convinced, he would be succeeded by one of his own sons. There was no room in Herod's world for a competing "King of the Jews." He had been given that title by the Roman Emperor himself. No one would take it away from him. The king's advisors informed him that, according to the prophet Micah, the Messiah was to be born in Bethlehem. They cited the prophet:

But you, O Bethlehem Ephrathah,
who are little to be among the clans of Judah,
from you shall come forth for me
one who is to be ruler in Israel,
whose origin is from old, from ancient days. (Micah 5:2)

Now the Wise Men were searching out the newborns whose birth synchronized with their celestial charts and calculations. Only under the scrutiny of their questions, did Mary's dream become known. She and Joseph reported all the things concerning their child. Then the Wise Men asked to see the holy child. Upon seeing him, the three Wise Men fell down before him and paid homage to the baby Jesus as to a king. Then, they opened their travelers' sacks and brought forth treasures of gold, frankincense and myrrh. These they presented to the holy family. Later when the holy family would flee into Egypt from the threat of King Herod, who tried to kill the baby Jesus, these valuable gifts would provide for them.

After the birth of Jesus in Bethlehem, Mary was considered 'unclean' for forty days according to temple law. After completing her time of purification, she could again enter the sacred courts of the Jerusalem Temple. Therefore when Mary's time of waiting was ended, Joseph and Mary took their firstborn up to Jerusalem to present the child at the holy Temple and offer the proscribed sacrificial offering to ransom their firstborn. How glad Mary was that day. She and Joseph would present the holy child in God's holy Temple. The dream was now very much alive. The difficult days of the past melted before the joy that possessed her as they ascended through the triple gate to the Temple Mount. Then they made their way across the wide expanse of the Court of the Gentiles to the sacred courts of the Temple. Surely, this would be a perfect day. What could possibly happen to the dream on this day of all days?

Then strange and troubling words were spoken concerning Mary and Mary's child. What could they mean? When Joseph and Mary entered the sacred Court of the Women, an old man in the Temple named Simeon approached them and blessed them saying,

"Behold this child is set for the fall and rising of many in Israel,
and for a sign that is spoken against
(and a sword will pierce through your own soul also)..."
(Luke 2:34b-35)

What a sword it would be! It would pierce the very heart and soul of Mary. Poor Mary! The joy of the first Christmas would become mingled with the great sorrow of Good Friday. The dream would only become reality through great suffering—both the suffering of Mary and Mary's son. At the heart of this dream, lay a dark shadow. It was the long and threatening shadow of a Roman cross. This dream would pierce Mary's heart as surely as Roman spikes would pierce the flesh of her son Jesus. Surely, Mary's Hebrew name 'Miriam' foreshadowed her sufferings. For her name means 'bitter myrrh' or 'bitter fragrance.' The flowering branches of the myrrh bush were covered with large branching and piercing thorns. Just so, the flowering of Mary's motherhood would be pierced with the bitter sorrow of Jesus' passion and death.

Yes, the dream was merging into reality, but the dream was permeated with a bitter fragrance of suffering. The dream, however, was not only Mary's dream. It was also God's dream, and Mary will play her part obediently and painfully to make the dream a reality. In the end, her dream—God's dream—would overwhelm the Herods, the Roman armies, and all who would resist it. In the end, the dream would become a powerful and world shattering reality. While Mary full of faith, blessed for her believing, would exclaim following Jesus' resurrection, "My son, my God!"

Chapter 1: Study Aids

Note: You may want to begin this session by reading together the first paragraph in the
Introduction.
1. What experience have any of us had with the Mary Tradition? Was it in the Catholic
Church?
2. What do you think the author means when he writes, "Those of us nurtured in Protestant devotion need to liberate Mary from the dusty attic of our own neglect, covered with the cobwebs of an inherited anti-Catholic bias against all things Catholic?" Is that a fair assessment of how Protestant Christians have dealt with Mary? What has been your experience?
3. What assumptions about Mary do we bring to this study? (You may want to list these on a large sheet of paper, so they may remain throughout this study.)
4. How do you respond to the author's statement, "To conceive the Son of God in her flesh was an easy thing, but to conceive him in her faith was considerably more demanding?"

5. How does Israel's dream of a coming Messiah help you understand what it meant for Jesus to be born in Bethlehem?

6. Why was the title "King of the Jews" used by the Wise Men considered subversive by Kind Herod?

7. Do we know why it was necessary for Joseph and Mary to present Jesus at the Temple and "ransom" him with an offering? (Note: After God delivered Israel from Egyptian bondage by killing all of the first born of Egypt, both human and live stock, God commanded the people to consecrate to God their fist born. "The Lord said to Moses, 'Consecrate to me all the first-born; whatever is the first to open the womb among the people of Israel, both of man and of beast, is mine.'" (Exodus 13:1-2). This event is commemorated at Passover.

8. In what sense does the author mean that Mary's dream is also God's dream?

9. As we close this session, join me in saying together a call to worship numbered 1, in Part II of this study book. Please disregard the seasonal references.

CHAPTER 2
MARY: A MODEL FOR ALL CHRISTIANS

"I am the Lord's servant," said Mary; "may it happen to me as you have said." (Luke 1:38) Most Protestant Christians have generally neglected Mary, the Mother of Jesus, and so
we have not seen Mary for what she truly is: *A model for all Christians.* Some of the Anglican tradition is a notable exception to this neglect, especially the Caroline divines of the seventeenth century. Yet it is surprising for most Protestant Christians to learn that the reformers of the sixteenth century wrote and spoke very highly of Mary. Martin Luther was emphatic about the divine motherhood. He wrote, "In this work whereby she was made the Mother of God, so many and such great good things were given her that no one can grasp them."[6] Although Luther did not support all that the Catholic Church taught about Mary, he returned to the subject of Mary frequently in his preaching and writing.

John Calvin wrote much less on Mary than did Luther, and his content was much more restricted. He reacted strongly to what he perceived to be gross distortions in Catholic practice regarding the veneration of Mary: "For Mary has been made Queen of Heaven, the Hope, the Life and the Salvation of the world, and, in fact, their insane raving went so far that they just about stripped Christ and adorned her with the spoils."[7] Still Calvin, in his biblical commentaries, speaks most highly of Mary. "Elizabeth called Mary Mother of the Lord, because the unity of the person in the two natures of Christ was such that she could have said that the mortal man engendered in the womb of Mary was at the same time the eternal God."[8] Again, Calvin urged upon us to take Mary as our teacher concerning faith. Commenting upon the text at the head of this chapter in which Mary obediently submitted to the divine summons, Calvin wrote, "We see then the instruction that is given to us here by the Virgin Mary, who will be to us a good teacher, providing that we take advantage of her lessons as it becomes us."[9] The Swiss reformer Ulrich Zwingli was closer to Luther in his views about Mary. He praised Mary saying, "I esteem immensely the Mother of God, the ever chaste, immaculate Virgin Mary."[10] Zwingli was against all invocation to Mary, but he kept the Hail Mary as a greeting and praise.

I believe we Protestant Christians, unfortunately, have overreacted to the *veneration* of Mary by our Catholic brothers and sisters. It is an ever common pitfall that when we react to what we perceive to be something that is one-sided, we often go too far to the other extreme. We over-react. Certainly, our reaction to Catholic Marian devotion is itself one-sided and fails to do justice to the biblical texts concerning Mary. Can we Protestant Christians recover a profound appreciation for Mary without accepting what we generally consider as excesses in Catholic Marian devotion? Perhaps it would be helpful to call attention to several of the later developments of Catholic doctrine concerning Mary that trouble many, if not most, Protestant Christians.

The doctrine of the "Immaculate Conception" of Mary was formalized in 1854. It taught that Mary "in the first instant of her Conception, by a singular grace and privilege granted by Almighty God, in view of the merits of Jesus Christ, the Saviour of the human race, was preserved free from all stain of original sin."[11] Thus, Mary was understood to be chosen for her divine vocation from before birth and conceived in a unique manner different from the rest of us mortals. The Eastern Church (Orthodox) does not accept this doctrine either, since that Church does not wish to separate the Blessed Virgin from the descendants of Adam and Eve. Then in 1950, the doctrine of the Assumption of Mary was fixed. "We pronounce, declare and define it to be a divinely revealed dogma: that the Immaculate Mother of God, the ever Virgin Mary having completed the course of her earthly life, was assumed body and soul to heavenly glory."[12] These more recent teachings of the Catholic Church concerning Mary have only served to estrange Protestant Christians further from any helpful assessment of Mary.

The most troubling of all the Catholic teachings about Mary may be, in fact, the oldest dogma of all—the perpetual virginity of Mary. Since Protestant Christians tend to put such great emphasis upon the biblical tradition, it is especially troublesome when a teaching about Mary is not only extra biblical but appears to contradict scripture. This is the case regarding the doctrine of the perpetual virginity of Mary. The Catholic Church teaches that Mary was not only a virgin when she conceived Jesus and a virgin when she bore Jesus, but she remained a virgin throughout her life including the time she was married to Joseph. This, for many Protestant Christians, seems to disparage the meaning and importance of matrimony and married love. However, the real stumbling block for many Protestant Christians regarding the doctrine of Mary's perpetual virginity is the clear witness of scripture where it refers to the brothers and sisters of Jesus.

The references to other members of Jesus' family are numerous and surprisingly include three from outside the Gospels. The Gospel references are listed here with parallel references in parentheses.

1. *"Is not this the carpenter, the son of Mary and brother of James and Joses and Judas and Simon, and are not his sisters here with us?" -Mark 6:3 (Matthew 13:55-56)*

2. *"And his mother and his brothers came; and standing outside they sent to him and called him." -Mark 3:31-32 (Matthew 12:46-50; Luke 8:19-20)*

3. *"After this he went down to Capernaum, with his mother and his brothers and his disciples..." -John 2:12*

4. *"So his brothers said to him, 'Leave here and go to Judea that your disciples may see the works you are doing'...For even his brothers did not believe in him." -John 7:3, 5*

These next three references to siblings of Jesus come from other writings in the New Testament, some of which may be older than the Gospel references.

1. Following the ascension of Jesus into heaven, the disciples along with other followers of Jesus returned from the Mount of Olives to the upper room in Jerusalem. Among those in the upper room we read,

"All these with one accord devoted themselves to prayer, together with the women and Mary the mother of Jesus, and with his brothers" (Acts 1:14).

2. The Apostle Paul refers to the married brothers of Jesus.

"Do we not have the right to be accompanied by a wife, as the other apostles and the brothers of the Lord; and Cephas?" (I Corinthians 9:5)

3. When the Apostle Paul went up to Jerusalem following his conversion to talk with the leaders of the Church, he informs us

that he talked with James the brother of Jesus, whom he called an apostle:

"But I saw none of the apostles except James the Lord's brother."

(Galatians 1:19)

The weight of evidence for the brothers and sisters of Jesus is overwhelming. Catholic interpreters have attempted to explain this discrepancy to their doctrine of Mary's perpetual virginity by various means. Some suggest that these siblings were children of Joseph by a former marriage. Others have claimed that they were actually cousins and not brothers. Besides the clear references to brothers and sisters of Jesus, there are other biblical passages that seem to suggest Mary was not a perpetual virgin, but rather lived in a normal state of matrimony with her husband Joseph.

1. We read, for example, that Joseph "knew her not until she had born a son." This seems to be saying that *until* the birth of Jesus, Mary remained a virgin. However, after she gave birth to Jesus, Joseph *knew* his wife Mary. Of course, the Bible in both testaments uses the Hebrew idea "to know" as a way of referring to sexual relations, as in "Adam knew his wife Eve and she bore a son."

2. In another place we read, "She [Mary] gave birth to her first-born son." Why "first-born" if the writer really meant only born? "First-born" suggests that there were other-born. It seems highly unlikely that the Gospel writers would have used such expressions as "until" and "first-born," if they assumed Mary was a life long virgin. Therefore, Protestant Christians are not troubled without some basis when we approach Mary in the Tradition. Nevertheless, we need to get past these hurdles and be true to our own Protestant tradition and come fresh to the biblical text to hear the Word of God.

To this end, I want to retell the biblical story of Mary's visitation by the angel Gabriel. As is my usual custom, I not only want to do serious work on the text. I want to come to the text with a creative and baptized imagination and try to 'flesh out' the story, as it were. Therefore, I will try to retell the story from the inside as I can imagine Mary may have felt and experienced it.

Now Mary, a simple and pious Jewish young woman about thirteen or fourteen years old, was devoutly praying her prayers in the enclosed courtyard of her modest home in Nazareth. Suddenly and without any expectation, an angel appeared to her. The angel's name was Gabriel. Mary was startled and afraid, both for the suddenness of the interruption and the appearance of the angel as a young man. In those days, a young woman sheltered from the outside world and carefully guarded to ensure her marriageability, would be just about as startled from the appearance of a man in her little courtyard as by a heavenly being. No wonder Mary was troubled. "Why is he here, and what could he possibly want with me?" Mary thought.

The angel, sensing Mary's distress, tried to reassure her.

"Don't be afraid, Mary, for God has been gracious to you," the angel said seeking to put her at ease. Of course, Mary knew already that God had been gracious to her, for God had been gracious to Israel. Her piety did not limit her view of God's graciousness simply to her own little world. The stories of her ancient Jewish tradition had opened to her a larger world than she had hardly known personally.

"What do you mean that God has been gracious to me?" Mary asked the heavenly messenger.

The angel answered, "God wants you to have a baby."

"I hope so," Mary said to herself. No woman in Israel would want to be childless. Such women were stigmatized as 'barren,' and their condition was considered a judgment of God upon them. Of course, Mary wanted to have a baby—someday.

"But God wants you to have this special baby right away," interrupted the angel, having read Mary's thoughts.

"Right away! Now I'm a simple peasant girl," replied Mary, starting to feel uncomfortable at the direction this conversation was taking, "but even I know that virgin girls do not have babies, and I won't be living with Joseph until after the betrothal period has ended."

"Oh, God can arrange that," replied the angel. "The Holy Spirit will overshadow you, and God's power will rest upon you."

"I believe that God can do anything," countered Mary. "But do you realize what you are asking of me?" she asked the angel. "God wants me to have a baby that has no father. Joseph will divorce me. What will my father say? It will kill my mother! I won't be able to hold up my head in Nazareth. The child won't stand a chance. How will I support him? You must be crazy!"

Mary pondered for a moment, then spoke, "Is this some kind of a testing?" Mary mused for a moment on that thought. "That's it! God doesn't want me to have a baby out of wedlock. God just wants to see how much I am willing to trust God. When I say 'Yes,' then you will tell me the real reason for your visit. Now I understand!" Mary seemed satisfied in her new assurance.

"Wait a minute," interrupted the angel, trying to get a word in edge-wise once the imagination of a thirteen year old girl gets started.

"I am afraid you do not understand, Mary. This is not a test in the way you think. God has chosen you to bear God's Messiah into the world. Your son will be called 'Son of the Most High God.' This child will be so special that God is doing this one in a special way. You could say God will be his father. You,

Mary, have been favored by God for this unique motherhood. God is asking you to carry God's only begotten Son within your womb." Then the angel stopped speaking and waited, looking carefully at the troubled young woman before him. She was so young.

Mary no longer found her words easily. Suddenly the weight of the angel's message pressed upon her from all sides. She could hardly get her breath. She felt faint.

"Could this really be?" Mary pondered, turning over the angel's words in her mind.

"Is the great and living God of Abraham and Sarah, Isaac and Rebekah, Jacob with Leah and Rachel—is this God—choosing me for some special divine favor? Is this some unique and special blessing for which God has singled me out, as when God singled out the barren Sarah in her old age to bear Isaac, the child of promise? Is it like the time God chose Esther for a special mission to save God's people? Could I be so chosen and so special?" Mary wondered, her mind beginning to race again. Finally, Mary spoke.

"Are you asking me or telling me?"

"Asking," Gabriel replied.

Mary's confidence began to return at the angel's answer.

"Well, I would be honored to oblige God's request. I have only a couple little requests of my own."

"Yes," said the angel, "and what would they be?"

"Well, first I want you to make this all public so everyone will understand and not accuse me of unfaithfulness to Joseph."

"No, I can't do that," said the angel.

"Well, then go explain it to Joseph, so he will know the truth and not divorce me."

"No, I can't do that either," said the angel again.

Now in desperation, Mary almost shrieked at the angel, "At least will you tell my mother?" Again, the angel replied, "No, I can't do that."

Panic began to grip Mary.

"Can't you do something, anything to help? All I'm asking for is just a little support here. I can't do this all by myself. You are an angel; you don't understand. I can bear the shame, the humiliation, and the suspicion. However, if Joseph divorces me, there is no way we can pull this off. We've got to bring Joseph along."

"Well, you explain it to Joseph. He loves you. He will understand," advised Gabriel.

"Believe me," replied Mary, "it will take an angel to convince Joseph that this baby, which is not his, is really fatherless."

"Alright!" said the angel, as Mary sank in exhausted relief, "I will visit Joseph in a dream and command him to complete his marriage to you—for the child's sake. By the way," said the angel, almost casually, "your relative Elizabeth, who is married to the old priest Zechariah, is no longer barren. She is already in her sixth month. I visited them also as part of this divine plan. However, stubborn old Zechariah would not believe me because of their advanced years, so I struck him speechless until his son is born. You may want to visit her. I suspect you two will have lots to talk about."

Then Mary knelt before God's messenger and said, with her heart full of faith, "I am the lord's servant; may it happen to me as you have said." Mary, full of obedient faith, simply and unreservedly submits herself to the divine will.

Mary's submission to God's will, which for Mary was a costly and precious thing, is reminiscent of Jesus in the garden of Gethsemane on the night he was betrayed. Jesus prayed,

"Father, if you will, take this cup away from me. Not my will, however, but your will be done" (Luke 22:42). As Jesus' life was darkened by the looming shadow of a Roman cross, he prayed for deliverance. Yet, he willingly submitted to the divine will. Likewise, Mary foresaw much of the danger and difficulty that faced her when she said: "...may it happen to me as you have said." She found great courage in the assurance of the angel, "The Lord is with you!" Mary would not face the future alone.

Hearing once again this remarkable story of Mary, we are reminded of the tension between God's good news and the bad news we find in it. Like Mary, we are called to live our lives in the midst of that tension. Mary can only reach out to embrace the good news of God's favor bestowed upon her by also embracing the tragic human consequences she and her family would suffer. Like Mary, we are summoned to find obedience there, to find our freedom there, to live our lives faithfully there. We are called to live graciously in that tension, called to live grace-filled lives in the midst of suffering, even innocent suffering, just as Mary did. For the arena of our Christian responsibility lies within the circle of tension between the good news and the bad news, between what God wants and what it may require of us.

Mary received the word of God from the angel Gabriel. God's messenger came uninvited and unexpected into Mary's quiet little world. We, too, need to be looking and listening for God's messengers. They, too, may come into our lives unexpected, even uninvited. How will we recognize them? They will call us to new faithfulness. They will not tell us what we want to hear, but what God wants us to hear. The power of that word may well thrust us out into the very tension and dangers we would wish to avoid.

God is forever seeking to become enfleshed in human life. God both summons us and allows us to share in that enfleshment. Mary played a unique role in the whole drama of God's enfleshment. Mary enfleshed God both in her body and in her faith. Mary allows herself to share the pain of God for the sake of God's enfleshment. In this way, Mary's will is taken up and transformed into God's will. In so doing, Mary has become a model for all Christians in the journey of faith.

Chapter 2: Study Aids

Note to Leader: If you can get a copy of any picture of the annunciation, when the angel came to Mary, have it on display as group members arrive. You may want to leave it up at lease for several weeks.
1. In what sense is Mary "a model for all Christians?"
2. Let's review what the Protestant Reformers said about Mary. (Review that section of the chapter.) How surprised were you to read the extent the Reformers revered Mary?
3. Protestant Christians do not tend to speak of veneration." However, veneration of Mary is part of Catholic piety. What comes to mind when you hear that Catholics venerate Mary?

Does it help to know that 'venerate' means "to admire or revere?" It dos not mean adoration or worship.

4. Let's review several Catholic teachings regarding Mary that are generally troubling to many Protestant Christians. a) the Immaculate Conception; b) the Assumption of Mary; c) the Perpetual Virginity of Mary. (Review this section of the chapter.) After each teaching is reviewed ask, "How do you respond to this

teaching?" Any questions or comments?

5. Let's review the biblical witness that contradicts any notion that Mary was perpetually a virgin. (Review this section of the chapter.) What is your reaction to this biblical evidence?

6. What, if anything, strikes you as you hear once again the story of Mary's visitation by the angel Gabriel?

7. How do you respond to Mary's question to the angel, suggested by the author, "Are you asking me or telling me?"

8. The author writes of "the tension between God's good news and the bad news we find in it." How to you respond to this claim of tension?

9. How does it strike you when the author claims that like Mary "We, too, need to be looking and listening for God's messengers?"

10. Let us close this session by saying together responsively a Sending Forth numbered 6 in Part II of this study book.

CHAPTER 3
"HAIL MARY, FULL OF GRACE"

"For behold, henceforth all generations will call me blessed..." (Luke 1:48b)

Many of us Protestant Christians are aware of the practice of Catholic Christians praying the Hail Mary.

Hail Mary, full of grace,
the Lord is with thee.
Blessed art thou among women,
and blessed is the fruit of thy womb, Jesus.
Hail Mary, Mother of God,
prayer for us sinners now
and at the hour of our death. Amen

Unfortunately, many of us Protestants have not had the privilege of participating in this reverential act of praying the Hail Mary with our Catholic brothers and sisters. I have had this privilege twice at a viewing or wake for deceased persons with a service at the close of the viewing.

The Hail Mary is in two parts. The first part simply celebrates the Virgin Mary because she is blessed by God to be the Mother of our Lord Jesus. Protestant Christians would have no trouble with that celebration. Our problem tends to be with the second part of the Hail Mary that makes a prayerful petition and invocation to Mary asking her to pray for us. It should be noted this second part was not originally part of the Hail Mary. It first appeared in print in 1495 and was added to the "Catechism of the Council of Trent" in 1566. The Council of Trent, as you can see by the date it met, was the Catholic Church's reactionary Council which met to stave off the rapid spread of the Protestant Reformation which was spreading from country to country in the first half of that century. The Council of Trent adapted a very anti-Protestant stance that only served to solidify the growing polarity in the Church. The Second Vatican Council, 400 years later, served to move the Church beyond Trent to a more ecumenical stance.

It should be further noted that the invocation to Mary in the second half of the Hail Mary is not supported or practiced in the Greek Orthodox Church. While they have a lively Marian devotion, they do not make as much use of the Hail Mary as is done in the Western (Latin) Church. They say the Hail Mary in the following manner.

Theotokos Virgin, Hail, Mary full of grace,
the Lord is with you.
Blessed are you among women,
and blessed is the fruit of your womb,
for you have born the Savior of our souls.

Notice the Greek Church's version of the Hail Mary does not include a prayer to Mary. Here is another example where the Western Church has added to the Tradition while the Eastern Church has rejected it.

Generally, we Protestant Christians have disagreed with our Catholic brothers and sisters in their veneration of the Virgin

Mary. For many, if not most of us, it seems like too much attention and veneration is shown to Mary that should be reserved for Jesus. We Protestants have also tended to avoid such expressions as 'Mary, Mother of God.' Certainly, most of us would never think of praying to or through Mary. As Protestants, we have been leery of any veneration of Mary that would tend to raise her somehow into the constellation of the Trinity. We have clearly rejected some of the major teachings of the Catholic Church about Mary.

For example, we in the Protestant tradition generally do not believe in the Immaculate Conception, which declares that Mary was somehow miraculously conceived so that she, unlike the rest of us, "was preserved free from all stain of original sin." We also have rejected the doctrine of Mary's Assumption bodily into heaven, which holds that the Virgin Mary "having completed the course of her earthly life, was assumed body and soul to heavenly glory." Since all Protestant Christians place primary importance upon scripture, we also have denied that Mary was perpetually a virgin. The scripture clearly refers to the brothers and sisters of Jesus, and even names at least some of them.

I say all of this about our negative Protestant views concerning such Catholic teachings about Mary, the Mother of our Lord, for a purpose. It is not my intention to bash our Catholic sisters and brothers. My purpose is to demonstrate that we Protestant Christians have been rather emphatic and vocal concerning what we do not believe about Mary. Unfortunately, I believe this negativism has led most Protestants to a general disregard for and neglect of Mary altogether. *We Protestants are quite clear what we do not believe about Mary, but we remain quite vague concerning what we do believe about Mary.* There is a deafening silence about Mary in many Protestant churches. We have tended to over-react to Catholic veneration of Mary and swing too far the other way, showing a general disregard and neglect of Mary, the Mother of our Lord.

We Protestant Christians have done Mary an injustice. For fear of venerating Mary too much, we have not venerated her at all. In the Protestant tradition, one hardly is aware of Mary in our liturgies. Oh at Christmas time, her name comes up occasionally in the carols we sing. How could we possibility avoid that? That is just my point! The place of Mary and her rightful place of importance in the Church has been secured in our Christian Tradition. The Bible itself has guaranteed Mary's place of importance. Yet, we Protestant Christians have generally been hesitant to take our rightful place among the generations who will henceforth call Mary blessed as is prophesied in the Song of Mary known as the Magnificat (Luke 1:46-55).

Whenever there is an assigned passage of scripture in the lectionary concerning Mary, Protestant pastors have generally taken that occasion to look away from the biblical text and preach about family life or sexual purity. It is as if we were saying with the ancients still, that the sole meaning of a woman's life is to look beautiful and to bear children. Now there is nothing wrong with those. However, they do not capture the essence of a human being who happens to be female. Neither do they summarize Mary for us.

Hail Mary, full of grace,
the Lord is with thee.
Blessed art thou among women,
and blessed is the fruit of thy womb, Jesus.

Most Protestant Christians, I believe, would be comfortable with this version of the Hail Mary.

Can we in good faith as Protestant Christians restore Mary to her proper importance as the Mother of our Lord Jesus Christ in the Christian tradition among us? Can we peel away the centuries of suspicion and bias surrounding this most fascinating and remarkable woman? Can we open our minds and clear our vision for a fresh look at Mary, the Mother of our Lord Jesus? If we can do this, it will not mean that we will accept *all* that the Catholic Church has taught about Mary. It will mean that we may see her in new ways, fresh ways, since we will no longer be filtering our vision and understanding of Mary through an inherited anti-Catholic bias.

I am simply asking us, at this point, to take a fresh look at Mary as she is portrayed in the Bible, apart from any other sources of the Mary Tradition. For my part, my own discovery of Mary has come from a serious study of the assigned scripture lessons concerning the nativity of our Lord, which we read each year in church on the third Sunday in Advent. This concentrated and serious struggling with the texts concerning Mary began for me in about 1982. There was no particular reason for this beginning. It just happened. I found myself getting excited at discovering Mary in the text of scripture, a Mary who can well be considered a model for all Christians.

Mary is a model not because of her virginity, even though that was a part of whom she was when God summoned her to obedience and service. Mary is a model for all Christians, I discovered, because of her great faith and obedience in the face of tremendous demands upon her young life. Here, I discovered, was a devout servant of God who could teach me much about faithfulness to God and God's word.

Hail Mary, full of grace,
the Lord is with thee.
Blessed are thou among women,
and blessed is the fruit of they womb, Jesus.

In our attempt to recover a true and balanced view of Mary, it will be appropriate for us to avoid sentimentality. A proper appreciation for Mary and her place in the tradition can rightfully begin with a careful examination of the passages in the Bible concerning her. We heed Jesus' warning against letting our imagination run ahead of us. You recall on one occasion while Jesus was teaching, a woman in the crowd raised her voice and called out a blessing to him. "Blessed is the womb that bore you and the breasts that you sucked" (Luke 11:27-28). Then Jesus redirected her blessing saying, "Blessed rather are those who hear the word of God and keep it!" Of course, Mary was indeed so blessed. She had heard the word of God and kept it. Yet Jesus did not want her motherhood to get in the way of the gospel he preached. It is hearing and keeping the word of God that matters foremost, as we will see in the life of Mary.

Mary has a place in both the Church's creeds and its scriptures that can not be assailed. The Apostles' Creed declares that Jesus "was conceived by the Holy Spirit, born of the Virgin Mary." While the Nicene Creed also enshrines Mary, reminding the Church that Jesus "who for us men and for our salvation came down from heaven, and was incarnate by the Holy Ghost of the Virgin Mary, and was made man." It is on the basis of such solid creedal Tradition that the Catholic Church speaks of Mary's divine motherhood as the "Mother of God." Protestants, generally, have avoided such language. We are more apt to speak of the Mother of our Lord, or Mother of our savior, or simply Mother of Jesus.

The notion of Mary's divine motherhood was defined by the Church at the Council of Ephesus in 431. Twenty years later, the Council of Chalcedon spoke of the two natures of Christ in this way:

...one and the same Son, Our Lord Jesus Christ, the same perfect in Godhead and the same perfect in human nature, true God and true man, the same with a rational soul and body, consubstantial with

*the Father according to divine nature, consubstantial with us
according to the human nature, like unto us in all things except sin.*
Then the Council added these words:
*...indeed born of the Father before the ages according to
divinity, but, in the latest days, the same born of the
Virgin Mary, Mother of God, according to the humanity.*
Just over a century later at the second Council of Constantinople (553), the Church condemned an erroneous interpretation of Chalcedon stating clearly its meaning regarding the two natures of Christ, and it did this in terms of Mary.
*Or, if anyone calls her the mother of the man or the
mother of the Christ, as if the Christ were not God, but
does not confess that she is exactly and truly the Mother
of God, because God the Word, born of the Father before
the ages, was made flesh of her in the last days, and thus
the holy Synod of Chalcedon confessed her, let such a one
be anathema.*

It has always been the official position of the Christian Church, enshrined in the creeds, that Jesus was God the eternal Son and eternal Word enfleshed. So it is quite apparent, it seems to me, that it logically follows that Mary could quite appropriately be called the Mother of God (Theotokos). Karl Rahner, writing about the Church's praise of Mary's divine motherhood, also grounds that praise in this creedal affirmation "which really concerns and has more to say about the union of two natures in the unity of the one person of the Word of God than about Mary herself"[13] Because Protestant Christians have generally avoided the title Mother of God for Mary, even still I am a little uncomfortable in using it. Nevertheless, I understand the fundamental doctrine of the Incarnation of God in the man Jesus to be safe-guarded by such language. Rahner rightly appeals to all Christians to affirm Mary's divine motherhood, "To this day

Christians of all denominations are called to confess their belief in the divine motherhood of the blessed Virgin, with the whole of tradition, and the reformers of the sixteenth century, too"[14]

What then is the basis for a proper veneration of Mary, the mother of our Lord? When I speak of veneration, I do not mean, as Catholics also do not mean, adoration. When we venerate Mary; we do not adore or worship her. We admire her; we greatly respect her. We revere Mary as one of the redeemed and sanctified in heaven, who is very special because of her unique role in God's plan of salvation. The imminent Catholic theologian Karl Rahner reminds us of this important distinction between venerating Mary and adoring Mary. "The special honour paid to Mary as the Mother of God, which of course has nothing to do with adoration."[15]

Mary is blessed, first, because she was chosen by God to be the mother of our Lord Jesus. Through Mary, God would become one of us. Through Mary with her simple and unreserved obedience, the eternal God entered the stream of our human history as a human being. God came not as an adult but as a helpless and gentle child, mothered by Mary. Of all the women in human history, only Mary was so chosen. Only Mary was overshadowed by the Holy Spirit in this unique way, so that she conceived in her body and gave her human flesh to God.

Mary is blessed, secondly, because she believed the word God sent by the heavenly messenger. The angel Gabriel greeted Mary:
Hail, O favored one, the Lord is with you...Do not be afraid, Mary, for you have found favor with God. And behold, you will conceive in your womb and bear a son and you shall call his name Jesus.   (Luke 1:28, 30-31)
Mary gently reminds the angel of what is all too obvious to anyone but an angel. Such is impossible Mary explained, "since I do not know a man." Do I need to remind you that the Bible used such polite words to speak of more intimate matters?

The angel Gabriel explained to Mary how God planned to work this miracle:

*The Holy Spirit will come upon you,
and the power of the Most High will overshadow you,
therefore the child to be born will be called holy,
the Son of God. (Luke 1:35)*

Mary, full of simple faith and a pure heart, knelt down at the angel's words and with the total unconditional gift of herself said:

*Behold, I am the handmaiden of the Lord;
let it be to me according to your word. (Luke 1:38-39)*

Mary's belief is cast in stark contrast to the unbelief of the old priest Zechariah, the husband of Elizabeth. The angel Gabriel had also visited him while he was performing his priestly duties within the Holy Place of the Temple in Jerusalem. While praying at the golden altar of incense before the Holy of Holies, the angel announced to the old priest Zechariah that his wife Elizabeth, who was both old and had been 'barren,' would bear him a son. Because the old priest found the promise of the angel Gabriel too hard to believe, he was struck speechless until the birth of his son, John.

*The angel said to Zechariah:
I am Gabriel, who stand in the presence of God; and
I was sent to speak with you, and to bring you this
good news. And behold, you will be silent and unable
to speak until the day that these things come to pass,
because you did not believe my words which will be
fulfilled in their time. (Luke 1:19-20)*

Zechariah, in the wisdom of his mind, could not believe there could be a nursery on the geriatric ward. Mary, on the other hand, in the simplicity of her heart believed God!

*Hail Mary, full of grace,
the Lord is with thee.*

Blessed art thou among women,
and blessed is the fruit of thy womb, Jesus.

A third reason Mary is blessed is because she has become a model for all Christians. Mary is more than a model of a devoted and pious mother, as important as that is. She is more than a model of a virgin life preserved for the sanctity of marriage, as fundamental as that is. Mary readily gave herself to believe and obey the heavenly messenger. In this, we can see that Mary lived graciously. When the summons of God placed before her an unbelievable and shattering demand, Mary was full of faith. Who of us is not challenged by Mary's readiness to believe and obey God, regardless of its apparent foolishness or its cost? Looking at Mary, who of us does not see what it means to devote ourselves unreservedly to the will of God? Yes, Mary can become our teacher in many ways. For Mary stands tall among the giants of faith in the Holy Scriptures. Truly, Mary is a model for all of us to follow on our journey of faith.

A fourth reason Mary is blessed is because of the 'fruit of her womb.' When Mary was greeted by her kinswoman, Elizabeth said to her: "Blessed are you among women, and blessed is the fruit of your womb!" (Luke 2:43). At that point in time, Mary's conception by the Holy Spirit had already occurred. *It is God the Son whom Mary enfleshes in her own body that blesses Mary above all other women blessed with motherhood.* Karl Rahner rightly observes, "The divine motherhood of the blessed Virgin is therefore God's grace alone, and her own act, inseparably."[16]

In ancient Jewish thought, a woman's greatness was measured by the children she bore. However, with Mary it was not simply a physical motherhood. Mary, in a supreme act of devotion, has placed her whole self, body and soul, at the service of God. Mary allows her body to be sanctified for divine motherhood to bear the world's savior. It is Mary's obedience to the word of God that makes this divine fruit of her womb truly earn for Mary a blessing above all other women.

Hail Mary, full of grace,
the Lord is with thee.
Blessed art thou among women,
and blessed is the fruit of thy womb, Jesus.

Like Mary, we all need to be ready and listening for God's messengers. Their coming may be an intrusion into our ordered lives, just as it was an intrusion into the quiet and protected life of Mary. When God comes to us, there is little consideration for our ever expanding comfort zones. God's messengers will not always tell us what we want to hear. Certainly, for Mary to be told that God wanted her to have a baby out of wedlock was just about the last thing Mary, or any other young woman for that matter, would want to hear.

God's angels, God's messengers, will not tell us what we want but what God wants. God's angels will tell us what God expects and requires of us. They will call us to a new faithfulness. God's angels can come to us in the face of a family member, a friend, a colleague, a stranger, even an enemy. These angels come with a word from God, a word either of blessing or of judgment. In whatever ways and in whomever these angels come into our lives to speak a word of God, we will not be the same again. We will have to put on the line who we are and what we are, just as Mary did. We will learn new things about ourselves, and recall things we had long forgotten or buried inside of us.

Yes, all generations will call Mary blessed. I am pleased to be counted among those generations who down through the ages of the Church have both blessed Mary and called her blessed. My invitation to you is to join the company of those generations, in fulfillment of Mary's words in the Magnificat, "For behold, henceforth all generations will call me blessed" (Luke 1:48b).

Hail Mary, full of grace,
the Lord is with thee.
Blessed art thou among women,
and blessed is the fruit of thy womb, Jesus.

Chapter 3: Study Aids

1. Have any of us had the experience of praying the Hail Mary? If so, what was it like for you?
2. How do you respond to the author's claim "We Protestants are quite clear what we do not believe about Mary, but we remain quite vague concerning what we do believe about Mary?"
   (Suggestion: You may want to list on a note pad or chalk board what participants think we can believe about Mary.)
3. How often have you heard a Protestant pastor preach a sermon on the topic of Mary? I do not mean a sermon that refers to Mary, but actually preach a sermon on the topic of Mary.
4. How often have you heard Mary named in any of our liturgy or worship aids, other than hymns?
5. The author calls upon us to take "a fresh look at Mary, the Mother of our Lord Jesus." How can we do that?
6. In what sense does the author say Mary can be a model for all Christians? What is your response?

7. Let's review the Chalcedonian Definition of Christ's two natures. (Review this section from the chapter.) What strikes you in this Definition?

8. The Council of Chalcedon called Mary Mother of God. What does this mean and not mean? What was the Council attempting to do with this title for Mary? (Note the Karl Rahner quote regarding the purpose of Mary's divine motherhood.)

9. We come again to that troubling word veneration. Does the author help us understand the meaning of veneration and differentiate it from what it does not mean? (Review the chapter section.)

10. The author gives four reasons Mary is blessed and so is worthy of our veneration. Let's review them. (Review chapter section.) After each reason given, ask this question, "Does this make Mary worthy of our veneration?"

11. Let us close this session by saying together responsively a call to worship numbered 1 in Part II of this book.

CHAPTER 4
MARY, THE ONE FAVORED BY GOD

> *"And Gabriel came to Mary and said, 'Hail, O favored one, the Lord is with you!...And the angel said to her, 'Do not be afraid, Mary, for you have found favor with God.'"*
> (Luke 1:28, 30)

The angel Gabriel greeted the young, virgin, Mary of Nazareth, "Hail, O favored one, the Lord is with you!" The word translated 'Hail' means literally "rejoice." Mary is called to rejoice because she has been favored by God. She was favored by God for a very special purpose: To be the Mother of the descendant of King David who would be the "Son of the Most High" God. The favor of God is understood to describe the unique and privileged role Mary is asked to perform in conceiving and bearing God's Messiah. Later scholastic theology would speak of that favor as "a grace freely given."

Oh, to be a favored one! Who of us would not like that? We all have known at times, what it is like to be favored, haven't we? Perhaps some of our fondest memories include moments when someone favored us: favored us with a special honor, favored us with special attention, favored us with a special gift, favored us with affirmation and support, favored us with understanding and forgiveness, favored us with their love, favored us with just being there for us when we really needed someone. What a boost to our sagging egos and exhausted hearts, to be favored in some way. It certainly makes your day, maybe your week! We have all had such special experiences of being favored, have we not?

However, you know there is a flip side to this business of being favored. Who of us has not known the disappointment of not being favored—when we really expected it, or when we felt we really deserved or needed it? We know how we have been hurt by words spoken carelessly, when we were expecting praise or even encouragement. It is very unfortunate how words spoken carelessly or thoughtlessly can hurt and discourage us. Such words wound and alienate long after they are rashly spoken. Perhaps, we would truly be favored by God if God would slow down our careless speech and speed up our withered hearts. Then maybe our words, spoken carelessly or in haste, and our thoughtless reactions would not wound our sisters and brothers. May our words and our deeds truly show favor to one another.

Mary is called favored one' She is startled, troubled, and disturbed by the angel's greeting. Gabriel reassured her, "Do not be afraid, Mary, for you have found favor with God." "Found favor"—does that mean the angel Gabriel has come to announce what has already happened? Has the Holy Spirit already overshadowed Mary and caused her to conceive in her womb the coming Messiah? Does the angel announce what God has already accomplished by the "Most High" overshadowing Mary? Instead, has the favor she has found with God mean that God has chosen Mary for this blessed purpose, but now Mary also must choose? God has chosen her, but does Mary have veto power? Can the divine plan for the salvation of the world be thwarted by a young Jewish woman only thirteen or fourteen years old? Can Mary actually say 'No' to Gabriel, a chief angel who stands before the living God and who reveals God's will and purpose for humanity? The biblical text is quite clear in its answer on this crucial point. The angel Gabriel announced God's plan to Mary, a plan that would vitally involve her and one that would shake Mary's life to her core. Nevertheless, at the point of the annunciation by Gabriel, it is only a plan. The angel said, "And behold you will conceive in your womb and bear a son..." The angel did not say to Mary, "You have conceived" but rather "you will conceive." Mary is chosen. She is not invaded! She is not violated! Mary will conceive if she consents to God's plan. Mary will not conceive if she rejects God's choosing. Mary must decide. That is an awfully big decision she must make at such a tender young age.

God has chosen. Now Mary must choose. Will she *allow* herself to be chosen by God? Will Mary become obedient to the heavenly vision? Will she say 'Yes'? Whatever Mary's answer to God's summons, it will cost her something. In fact, it will cost her much. Whether Mary says 'Yes,' or whether she says 'No,' Mary will never again be the same Mary she was before the angel Gabriel visited her. When God comes to us in both gift and demand, however we answer that summons, we can never be the same again. The hour of our visitation is always a tipping point in our lives. How could it be otherwise, to be encountered, to be summoned by the living God?

In the experience of Mary, we discover the nature of God's choosing, the manner in which God seeks to reveal the divine will and purpose in human life. God's choosing may be shattering and costly, as it was for Mary, but God's choosing is never manipulative, never autocratic, never devoid of grace. God's choosing is never forced upon us. God's choosing always comes to us as a gift, always seeks our compliance. That which can only be freely given can never be forced, and what is forced is not freely given.

How often do we confuse these two in our own choosing? What we choose, we may easily demand. What in the beginning is our choice may in the end become our demand. Such choosing, however, ceases to be a gift and an opportunity when it becomes our demand and our claim upon another person. It then becomes the invasion of our will into another person's life. What started out as only our wanting and choosing can degenerate into a battle of wills as we seek to impose our will upon another person, even upon someone we love. It is very easy to confuse our choosing with our so-called rights. We begin to think that, of course, our choosing is best; therefore, it must be accepted no matter what. That is when our choosing deteriorates into just another demand.

What we learn from the way God chooses Mary is this: No matter how worthwhile and how important is our choosing it cannot be forced upon another person without violating the dignity and freedom of that person. God, with a great and wonderful plan, still must send an angel to Mary asking for her consent. Certainly, God will not force Mary to do God's will, anymore than God forces any of us to do God's will. God's coming to us is never an invasion. It is always gracious. God's coming is always a grace-filled moment. We see that clearly in the way God came to Mary.

The future of God's plan for the whole human race is placed before this most unlikely candidate—a thirteen or fourteen year old, first century, Jewish young woman who still lives with her parents. What a surprise! What an unlikely person to play such a crucial role in the purposes of the Almighty. Men were usually the recipients of God's messages in Israel. Here is a woman, a humble virgin girl in her home in a small town in The Galilee.

A PROTESTANT DISCOVERS MARY

Mary was a 'nobody,' the daughter of a 'nobody,' who lived in an out-of-the-way, 'nobody' town. It is both amazing and wonderful that someone whom this world calls a 'nobody,' the living God calls a 'favored one.' You see, there aren't any nobodies in God's sight. In fact, God seems to get along just fine with the so-called nobodies of this world, such as the poor, the simple, the unemployable, the chronically ill, and the homeless. The list of the marginalized people goes on and on. There seems to be a special place in God's heart for these needy ones. Just as the Bible reports God's 'preferential option' for those who were most vulnerable and powerless in ancient Israel, such as the poor, the widow, the fatherless, and the alien.

The people God seems to have the most problems with, however, are those who think they are more than they really are. They become proud and haughty and distance themselves from their brothers and sisters whom they perceive to be different from them, even less than them. It is the rich and the powerful, the self-righteous, and the self-made folks who find it hardest to enter the Kingdom of God. Such folks often find it hard to be gracious or to receive grace. Those people who confuse worldly status and social acceptance with status before God, or those who confuse their worldly comfort with God's favor—those are the people who find it easiest to turn a deaf ear to God's choosing. Those people must struggle most to say 'Yes' to God in the hour of their visitation. Is it any wonder then that God chose Mary instead of the daughter of a prince of Judah or even King Herod's daughter? Only someone as simple as Mary would be surprised to be called favored one.

God's choosing, to be favored by God can be shattering just as it was for Mary. Her whole future and promise were bound-up in her 'marriageability,' as it was for all such first century peasant Jewish women. Only by preserving her sexual innocence was

Mary likely to receive a satisfactory offer of marriage. After her betrothal, as was the custom, Mary still lived with her parents for one year. This was an important trial period. If anything were amiss in the bride's background—translate that: If she were not a virgin—, it was to be discovered during this betrothal period.

Certainly, it was an act of grace for Mary's benefit that God's plan for her conception came in the latter part of that one year trial period. Joseph could still divorce her quietly if he chose. Joseph, instead, could complete the marriage and take his bride home with him. So Matthew reports, "When Joseph woke from sleep, he did as the angel of the Lord commanded him; he took his wife…" (1:24). By taking Mary home with him, Joseph officially ended the trial period and claimed the child as his own. Mary's secret could be kept for awhile at least. However, God's choosing will bring to the innocent Mary, to her family, and to Joseph only scorn and shame. For now, there would be for Mary much pain and little glory in saying 'Yes' to God's choosing.

Mary, filled with wonder and with much trepidation, commits herself. "Behold I am the handmaiden of the Lord…" Then those fateful words that will fill her life with terrible anguish, Mary answers, "Let it be to me according to your word." Can we imagine how frightening was such a commitment for Mary? With it would come humiliation and shame. With her commitment, there would also be the possibility of death by stoning for being found pregnant during her betrothal. Mary's 'Yes' to God was a costly consent. It would even cost her more than her young innocent mind could then imagine.

The consecration of Mary to God's purpose and what it will mean for her appears well embodied in a prayer that is part of the United Methodist Church's Wesleyan heritage. It is the Covenant Prayer in the John Wesley Covenant Service. In a church where I was pastor, we prayed this prayer during a covenant service on the first Sunday of each New Year. Pray this prayer very deliberately, and you will see how clearly it expresses the costly nature of God's choosing, a choosing which would come to clutch the very soul of Mary.

> Lord, make me what you will. I put myself fully into your hands: put me to doing, put me to suffering, let me be employed for you or laid aside for you, let me be full, let me be empty; let me have all things, let me have nothing. I freely and with a willing heart give it all to your pleasure and disposal.[17]

That is the response to God's choosing of all those saints down through the ages who have found in God's choosing their perfect freedom, their health, and their salvation. It was the response of Mary, who could see quite clearly the costliness of God's grace upon her life. May it be our own response to God's choosing in the hour of our visitation, when we discover that we, too, have been favored by God.

CHAPTER 4: STUDY AIDS

1. Do you recall moments in your life when you were favored by someone? What was it like?
2. The author reminds us that Mary was chosen by God, but now she must choose. How does that alter, in any way, your appreciation for Mary since she also had to choose?
3. How do we allow ourselves to be chosen? (Perhaps other biblical examples of God's choosing would be helpful, e.g. Moses, Jeremiah, Abraham, Esther.)
4. How does God's choosing, as demonstrated in Mary's life, help you understand the nature of your own choosing to favor someone? (Note: The author writes, "What we choose, we may easily demand.") What are some examples of choosing that becomes a demand?
5. The author writes, "It is both amazing and wonderful that someone whom this world calls a 'nobody,' the living God calls a "favored one."" What does this say to you about human dignity?

Have you had the experience when a seeming nobody, one of the marginalized people, suddenly touched you with their dignity? Would you share that moment with us?

6. How do you understand what the author calls God's "preferential option" for those who are poor and vulnerable?

7. The author writes, "God's choosing, to be favored by God can be shattering just as it was for Mary." How does the idea of God's choosing becoming a shattering experience deepen your understanding of being chosen or favored?

8. Introduce the John Wesley "Covenant Prayer." Have any of us experienced this prayer in a worship setting? If so, what was the occasion? (Ask the group to pray, not say, this prayer together.)

9. How do you respond to what this Covenant Prayer is saying?

10. Join with me as we close this session by saying responsively a Sending Forth numbered 6 in Part II in this study book.

CHAPTER 5
'WHY DID THIS HAPPEN TO ME?'

*"Why should this great thing happen to me,
that my Lord's mother comes to visit me?"*
(Luke 1:43 in The New Testament In Today's English Version*)*

The angel Gabriel reassured the troubled Mary by promising her a sign. Her relative Elizabeth, who had remained childless into her old age, had miraculously conceived and was now in her sixth month. Mary quickly arranged to travel to the hill country of Judea to see this marvelous sign. For the angel declared to Mary: "For with God nothing will be impossible." With great haste the young virgin named Mary, who became miraculously pregnant according to the word of the angel, visited Elizabeth, who in her old age was miraculously pregnant and who had remained in hiding for the first five months. Now Mary would go to her and see this great thing for herself. The child of Elizabeth's old age would be the mighty prophet John the Baptist. John would go before Jesus, Mary's child, to bear witness to him that Jesus was the Messiah. With great joy, Elizabeth greeted Mary, and the babe leaped in her womb the Bible says in recognition of the Messiah's mother.

"'Why should this happen to me?'" That was the question Elizabeth asked Mary at their greeting. It is the question we often ask ourselves. What comes to mind when you hear that question? I suspect our thoughts turn more to the tragic side of life than to its goodness. We generally ask that question when we are facing hardships, injustices, sufferings and the like. We are more often likely to ask it when we were passed over for a promotion than when we got one. We are more likely to ask it when we have received bad news than good news. Underlying the question is the notion that we did not deserve what has happened. After all such thinking runs, people ought to get what they deserve in life! When something good happens to us, we generally feel that we deserve it. So, the question of 'Why?' gets raised mostly on the deficit side of life's ledger.

That was the kind of thinking expressed by Jesus' disciples upon seeing a blind man who sat by the road begging. The beggar was known by them to be blind since birth. "Rabbi," the disciples asked Jesus, "who sinned, this man or his parents, that he was born blind?" (John 9:2). Jesus answered them, "It was not that this man sinned or his parents..." On another occasion, Jesus cited a local tragedy in which eighteen people were killed when a tower collapsed in Jerusalem. He asked:

"Of those eighteen upon whom the tower in Siloam fell and killed them, do you think they were worse offenders than all the others who dwelt in Jerusalem? I tell you, No..."
(Luke 13:4-5)

Jesus rejected all such pat answers for tragedy and innocent suffering. Life does not come to us according to what we deserve. It just comes to us. Ours is an imperfect world in which evil sometimes prospers—but only for a season!—while the innocent suffer.

Must we see in our question of 'Why?' only the dark side of life? Truly, we are children of our age, seared by the daily reports of tragedy near and far. However, the question asked by Elizabeth comes from the other side—not the dark side but the bright side. It is the question of Elizabeth when she was greeted by Mary, who had come to visit her. "Why should this great thing happen to me...?" she asked. Elizabeth reminds us that we are often just as undeserving of the many good things that happen to us as we are of the wrongs that we suffer. After all, do we not know that nearly all if not all of the most important things in our lives comes to us as sheer gifts: the love of a spouse, the blessings of children, the support of a friend, the forgiveness of someone we hurt, a welcome among strangers, and the list can go on.

Life at its most profound level always comes to us as gift. Throughout our lives, we have been encouraged to become gift givers, but the thing that troubles many of us is how to become gracious gift receivers. I have found that good people are not always comfortable recipients of gifts. Watch how evasive we become receiving a simple compliment. Good folks are comfortable in *giving* gifts. We need to face up to the fact that all the truly important relationships in our lives come to us without merit. We do not and we can not deserve them. We can only receive them with a gracious spirit. Elizabeth had such a gracious spirit. She was touched by the gift of Mary's visit and the news she received concerning Mary's child. Whether blessings or sufferings come to us, however, faith hears in both of these a summons. Not that God is necessarily the prime mover—the cause—of what happens to us. Nevertheless, faith looks always and everywhere for God's summons to obedience and service. Even in our suffering.

Faith can hear God's summons to obedience and service in the most unlikely places. Take for instance Mary, the Mother of our

Lord. God summoned Mary to a special mission, to bear in her young body the Son of the Most High. And she unwed! What a tragedy to be an unwed mother in first century Israel. What a tragedy any time and anywhere. What shame! What stigma! I remember when as pastor I would receive a telephone call from a distraught mother asking me to come over and see her right away. She did not volunteer any information over the phone; however, the sound in her voice revealed she was terribly upset. I asked what was the matter, and she said she would tell me when I got there. My mind quickly ran down the possible reasons for her anxiety. If there had been a serious accident or death, she would have told me. What could be so upsetting, yet she could not tell me over the phone? I decided it must be that her teenage daughter was pregnant. When I arrived at the woman's home, I found my conjecture was correct. There are not that many things that will upset a mother or father more, besides a tragic accident or death, than discovering their daughter or son is about to become an unwed parent.

What virgin maiden would volunteer for the mission for which God had summoned Mary—even to bear the Son of God? By faith, Mary freely submits herself to the divine plan. She will lend her body to give human life to God, to enflesh God in the world. Yet, she must agree to accept this summons and begin her gracious task while she is still unwed. Only she could possibility know for certain. Only she could know that she had remained faithful to her betrothal vows with Joseph. Only she could know that growing in her body she carried and would birth the divine Savior of the world. It would take an angel to convince Joseph!

God had summoned Mary. She was to be God's partner in ushering in the day of salvation. Who would possibly believe her? It would be just as hard then for people to believe the report of Mary, as it would be now. That kind of thing just did not happen and does not happen. Not in this world! We all know that don't we? Yet it did happen. The merciful and all gracious God chose to become enfleshed in our existence, in our history, and live among us in our vulnerability. God needed a special woman to serve as the portal, the gateway of God's coming. God choose the young and innocent Mary. To which she could well cry out, 'Why me?'

The Bible does not say that we should seek out suffering. There is neither biblical truth nor virtue in that. There are three kinds of trouble noted Ralph Sockman, who was for many years pastor of a great New York City church. There is trouble we can avoid. There is trouble we cannot avoid, and there is trouble we must not avoid. If standing fast for our faith means that we are criticized, if being faithful in our service means we experience some inconvenience, if being co-workers with God requires us to sacrifice, then those things fall under the heading of 'Trouble we must not avoid." Mary was faced with a trouble she must not avoid. Mary, in order to be faithful to God and to herself, must take upon herself the suffering and indignities that will come with consenting to incarnate God in her virgin womb.

In addition to Mary, another striking example of the way faith hears God's summons to obedience and service in the most unlikely places is our Lord's death on the cross. Now here are all the trappings of a full blown tragedy. Here was an itinerant preacher traveling about the countryside and proclaiming the Kingdom of God, teaching people to love and forgive, and healing the sick. Then they crucified him. To the eye of the sophisticated and wise, the cross of Jesus was his tragic defeat. Pontius Pilate certainly thought so. It readily appeared to the most objective of observers that God had been defeated on that first Good Friday. The dream of God seemed to flow down from the cross of Jesus and disappear into the earth just as did Jesus' life that day. Whatever God may have wanted to accomplish in the life of Mary's son, it all seemed to have ended at 3 P.M. Jerusalem time on a Roman cross at Golgotha. This troublesome Jesus was now silenced for good—for ever! Only faith hears in this awful and senseless death the summons of God, a summons to new life, to life beyond death, to resurrection.

In the life of Mary, we discover also that in the good that comes to us faith hears the summons of God. Unfortunately, we Protestants Christians have generally overlooked the importance and place of Mary in our Christian tradition. The seemingly excessive importance given to Mary by our brothers and sisters in the Catholic Church has led to our own extreme position—an unnecessary neglect of one who can only be called the first disciple.

Mary received a great blessing. God had summoned her to be the mother of the Messiah. There is no adequate explanation to the question, "Why Mary?" God needed a helper. Mary, like no doubt many other maidens in Israel, was a likely candidate. So God chooses. Moreover, God's choosing is a summons—a summons, not to privilege, but a summons to obedience. Such obedience may also lead to suffering, even to great suffering. Thus, it was with Mary. Besides the suffering and humiliation that she must endure having conceived out of wedlock, Mary would lose her firstborn who one day would be tragically executed on a cruel Roman cross. Anyone who visits St. Peter's in Rome and stands before that magnificent sculpture of Mary cradling in her arms the dead body of her son is moved by Mary's suffering and loss. Michelangelo, in that great work known as the *Pieta*, has captured the pathos of that tragic but tender moment following the crucifixion of Jesus.

The cross always stands at the center of God's choosing. Suffering for righteousness sake has a strange redeeming, healing quality. God's righteousness is strengthened in the world whenever we are enlisted on its side, in its defense, at all costs. The hand of God for establishing the Kingdom of God is strengthened by every single act of faithfulness. Mary's one act of saying 'Yes' to God would help unleash an ever growing flood of people saying 'Yes' to God. When Mary said her 'Yes' to God, she could not know, just as we cannot know, what would be the full consequences of her faithful obedience. It was not given to Mary to know with any assurance what the future of her actions would mean. She was summoned to serve God with her whole self, at the moment of God's call without knowing the full measure of what it would cost her. Believe me it would cost her plenty. Nevertheless, God needed from Mary a readiness and willingness to trust God, even trust God with her future. Mary trusted the word of God enough to place her whole future and her whole life in God's hands. God asks of us nothing less.

Like Mary, we do not always see the results of our faithfulness. Only much later after the resurrection, when we find Mary among the post-Easter disciples in Jerusalem, do we learn that Mary was blessed to see the final and glorious results of her simple act of saying 'Yes' to God so many long and hard years before. Yet, every single act of faithfulness to God is a help to God in the struggle with evil in this world. Therefore, Mary breaks out in song: "My soul magnifies the Lord, and my spirit rejoices in God my Savior." Mary's song has come down through the ages of the Church. It has inspired generations.

How easy it is to focus upon Mary's beautiful song and miss Elizabeth's profound and moving question. While Mary's heart is over-flowing with the joy of saying 'Yes' to the God who summons her, Elizabeth simply asks, "Why am I so fortunate? Why am I getting to see all this? Why me?" Even in her old age, she too was nurturing a new life within her body. Yet, she was free to share Mary's joy, and not to take away from it. She was now doubly blessed. She felt undeserving on both counts. Truly, God is good! Elizabeth had discovered that. So had Mary! Can you picture the situation? Here is Mary, unable to have a child because she is a virgin, and with her is her elder relative Elizabeth, who was unable to have a child because she was 'barren.' When they greet each other, both of these women are pregnant. Boy did they have a lot to talk about!

Elizabeth's question was also Mary's question. Their question needs to become our question. The gracious spirit of that question is the proper spirit of all who are summoned to obey and serve God, who would become God's partners in the care and keeping of this world. In that question we find reflected the goodness and graciousness of life. Life with all its manifold and unnumbered blessings is sheer gift. Why are we so fortunate? Why do we so often get much more than we deserve? Because God is good. God is gracious. Because God does not come to us on the basis of what we deserve but rather on the basis of unconditional love for us and for all persons.

Chapter 5: Study Aids

1. When Elizabeth greets Mary, she asks, "Why should this happen to me?" What comes
to mind when you her that question? When do we usually ask it?
2. Underlying the question of 'Why' is the notion that people ought to get what they deserve in life. But life does not always come to us according to what we deserve. How does that help us grasp the meaning of grace?
3. Elizabeth's question reminds us that we are often just as undeserving of the many good things that happen to us as wee are the wrongs that we may suffer. What are some of these good things in our lives that we do not deserve?
4. The author suggests good people are better at giving gifts than they are at receiving gifts. What do you thin is meant by that?
5. Mary will have to suffer the stigma of being an unwed parent, if she says 'Yes' to God's summons. Even if Joseph still completes their marriage following the betrothal, the wags will do the math. What does this say about innocent suffering?

6. How do you respond to the author's claim that "It would be just as hard then for people to believe the report of Mary as it would be now?"

7. How do you react to Ralph Sockman's observation that there are 3 kinds of trouble: 1) trouble we can avoid; 2) trouble we cannot avoid; and 3) trouble we *must not* avoid? (Mary was faced with the third kind of trouble, the kind she must not avoid.)

8. Why would the author call Mary the "first disciple?"

9. The author writes, "Mary trusted God enough to place her whole future and her whole life in God's hands. God asks of us nothing less." How do we embrace such costly grace?

CHAPTER 6
MARY'S SONG: THE MAGNIFICAT

"My soul magnifies the Lord, and my spirit rejoices in God my Savior, for he has regarded the low estate of his handmaiden. For behold, henceforth all generations will call me blessed; for he who is mighty has done great things for me, and holy is his name. And his mercy is on those who fear him from generation to generation. He has shown strength with his arm, he has scattered the proud in the imagination of their hearts, he has put down the mighty from their thrones, and exalted those of low degree; he has filled the hungry with good things, and the rich he has sent empty away. He has helped his servant Israel, in remembrance of his mercy, as he spoke to our fathers, to Abraham and to his posterity for ever."
-Mary of Nazareth (Luke 1:46-55)

Albrecht Durer, in one of his woodcuts, gives us a magnificent picture of Mary as she is greeted by her older relative Elizabeth. It is called "The Visitation." Upon hearing from the angel Gabriel that her relative Elizabeth had conceived in her old age, Mary hurried from Nazareth to the hill country of Judea to visit her. We see the two women greeting each other with an embrace that is rather awkward because of their large bellies. There is Elizabeth, who is too old to have a baby, reaching out to the younger Mary, who is too young to have a baby. Each woman seems a bit uncomfortable by her own pregnancy and each is a bit surprised to see the other in the bloom of pregnancy. One can only imagine the emotions of that moment. Neither woman seems altogether settled into the new reality of her life.

Elizabeth is now in her sixth month, at the time Mary "went with haste into the hill country, to a city of Judah" to visit her relative. For the first five months of her pregnancy, Elizabeth hid herself saying, "Thus, the Lord has done to me in the days when he looked on me, to take away my reproach among men" (Luke 1:25). Her reproach was to have been barren all those years, unable to bear children for Zechariah. In her world, for a woman to be unable to bear children was a tragic disgrace. Now Elizabeth's miraculous pregnancy was so startling and frightening that she withdrew for the first five months. Now in her sixth month, Elizabeth has become a bit more confident and again returned to a more normal social routine. Was it Mary's visit that coaxed Elizabeth from her sequestered existence?

Mary's pregnancy, however, would have just begun with her consent to God's plan as spoken by the angel. Therefore, Durer takes artistic license in picturing Mary as though she were in the last trimester of her pregnancy. Yet, what is pictured is none-the-less profound because the woodcut reminds us that the real meaning of the visitation is not just Mary's visit to Elizabeth, but rather the visitation of the angle to each woman. For in their heavenly visitation both Elizabeth and Mary were favored by God with the gift of their child. Mary was gifted with her child in her virginity, while Elizabeth was gifted with her child in her barrenness.

Mary stayed with Elizabeth, Luke reports, about three months. This would suggest that Mary was with Elizabeth through her delivery, or else Mary returned to Nazareth in The Galilee just before the birth of Elizabeth's son John. It is difficult to imagine that Mary would leave just at the time Elizabeth was to give birth, when Elizabeth would need her, and after Mary had already stayed so long with her. Elizabeth and Zechariah's son John would become the great prophet John the Baptist according to Luke's Gospel. At the greeting of Mary, Elizabeth breaks out in a canticle praising Mary and pronouncing this blessing: "Blessed are you among women, and blessed is the fruit of your womb!" Mary responds by praising God in a canticle of her own, which has become one of the great hymns of the Church, known as the "Magnificat," "My soul magnifies the Lord, and my spirit rejoices in God my Savior..." While Elizabeth praises Mary, Mary praises God. Characteristic of Mary's song is that she rejoices, not in what she will do or accomplish but in what God will accomplish and do in her and through her son.

Mary's song resounds with images and thoughts from the Hebrew Scriptures. It is almost a mosaic of Old Testament passages. The major allusions are to the Psalms and the Song of Hannah at the birth of her son, the prophet Samuel (I Samuel 2:1-10). Hannah had Sung, "My heart exults in the LORD; my strength is exalted in the LORD." Hannah's son Samuel, like Elizabeth's son John, became a great prophet in Israel. Samuel would anoint both Saul and later David as the first two kings of Israel. John will anoint Jesus at our Lord's baptism.

E. Stanley Jones, the great missionary to India, called Mary's song the Magnificat "the most revolutionary document in the world." The song of Mary refers to the "low estate of [God's] handmaiden." In this song, Mary associates herself with the memories of the 'poor ones' whom God helped by divine might. Whether they were barren women yearning for children, or Israel suffering under oppression and reduced to the status of a handmaiden, which was little more than a female slave or servant, the poor ones could look only to God for their help and their deliverance. Mary obviously identifies with the poor ones. She may have considered herself one of them.

This revolutionary song actually refers to three revolutions of God. There is a moral revolution. God "has scattered the proud in the imagination of their hearts" (vs. 51). Secondly, there is a social revolution. God "has put down the mighty from their thrones, and exalted those of low degree" (vs.52). Thirdly, Mary sings of an economic revolution. God "has filled the hungry with good things, and the rich he has sent empty way" (vs. 53). What God will accomplish through Mary's son will overthrow the very foundations of the world as it has been ordered by humanity. God will reorder the world according to justice, mercy and peace. It will be the new order of life in God's Kingdom.

Later Mary's son Jesus would come blessing the poor, the hungry, the downtrodden, and the persecuted.

Blessed are you poor, for yours is the kingdom of God.
Blessed are you that hunger now, for you shall be satisfied.
Blessed are you that weep now, for you shall laugh.
Blessed are you when…they exclude you and revile you and cast out your name as evil. (Luke 6:20-22)

Jesus kept table fellowship with tax collectors and sinners, whom society had excluded as outside the covenant community of Israel. He carried on an active ministry of healing, specifically to those who had been excluded from the promises of salvation by the

Holiness Code of the Jerusalem Temple. Those who were excluded were the lame, those with an issue of blood, and those who were believed to be possessed. Jesus even healed lepers who were excluded from society generally and excluded by the code from even entering the holy city of Jerusalem.

Jesus, however, did not only have blessings for the poor and oppressed. He also pronounced woes upon the rich, the full, those contented with things as they are, and those who have social status. Such persons seemed to have their ease, their wealth, and their reputations at the expense of the poor and the oppressed. So Jesus taught,

> *But woe to you that are rich for you have received your reward.*
> *Woe to you that are full now, for you shall hunger.*
> *Woe to you that laugh now, for you shall mourn and weep.*
> *Woe to you, when all men speak well of you,*
> *for so their fathers did to the false prophets.*
> *(Luke 6:24-26).*

We hear in both Mary's song and Jesus' blessings and woes what has been called God's "preferential option for the poor." God seems especially to be on the side of those who most need God on their side and who have no one else to plead their cause or protect them from the powerful and the privileged. Among them are the widows, the orphans, the landless, and the homeless sojourners. Now God's covenant with David will be fulfilled through the conception of God's Messiah in the handmaiden Mary. The dream of God's shalom will dawn upon the world through Mary's son. Shalom is a rich and many faceted word whose meanings includes peace, well-being, health, and wholeness.

There are those who believe that in her song Mary glorified in her virginity. Others say Mary glorified in her humility. She gloried in neither, said Martin Luther, but solely in God's gracious regard. Mary praises God who has "regarded the low estate of God's handmaiden," "exalted those of low degree," "helped his servant Israel," and "done great things to me." At this point, Mary appears no longer to be troubled and frightened as she was when the angel first unsettled her with the perplexing word of God. She seems now to be at peace with God's design and favor. Even though the problem of Joseph's reaction to her pregnancy does not yet appear to have been resolved.

Since Mary left for her visit to stay with Elizabeth in Judea shortly after the annunciation by the angel, there would have been no reason to tell Joseph about the angel's word to her before she left. Mary's first concern was to behold the marvelous sign promised by the angel in the miraculous pregnancy of Elizabeth. However, upon Mary's return after her three month visit with Elizabeth, the need to inform Joseph would have been both apparent and compelling. The honor of Joseph and his family would have required it. Upon being told of her pregnancy, sometime after Mary returned to Nazareth, Joseph could have chosen to do the honorable thing and divorce Mary quietly. However if Joseph had wished to follow the letter of the Law, he could have denounced Mary as adulterous, and she would have been tried before the Sanhedrin, as would her son many years later. Mary possibly could have been stoned to death by order of such a court.

The destiny of Mary as an individual becomes the symbol and the fulfillment of her people's vocation. Identity between Mary and Israel in its fullness is implicit in Mary's song, as it reaches towards a climax in the new Israel, which is the Church of God. Mary's song recognizes how God "has helped his servant Israel in remembrance of his mercy, as he spoke to our fathers, to Abraham and to his posterity for ever" (vs. 54-55). This larger sweep of God's blessing is reflected in Elizabeth's greeting when she says to Mary, "Blessed is the fruit of your womb!" Her words echo the promise of God to Israel when the wandering people were about to enter in and possess the land of promise. Through Moses, God reminded them to obey God by carefully doing all the commandments of God. If they would be faithful in keeping them, Israel would be greatly blessed. Among the many blessing listed there is the one echoed by Elizabeth, which God promised through Moses: "Blessed shall be the fruit of your body..." (Deuteronomy 28:4).

Yes, dear Mary's blessing is not a purely personal one. She has a role in God's plan for the destiny of God's people because Mary has conceived in her body the long awaited Messiah who will be the glory of Israel. This crucial role in the salvation of God has been made possible through both God's choosing and Mary's obedience. Sometimes, we lose sight of the larger sweep of God's plan and the purposes of God's blessings. We become quite satisfied to receive God's blessings for our own personal benefit and comfort. This tendency is so pervasive in our culture that we often confuse our own comfort, that has been grasped by our own hand, with God's blessings.

This confusion makes it even more difficult for us to relate to Mary's song, which comes in the midst of great distress, personal disgrace, and even danger to Mary. Her joy comes not in believing that God has enlarged her comfort zone, but rather in the confidence that God is working out the divine purpose on the landscape of history, even at the cost of great personal sacrifice for Mary. Here is nothing of the cheap grace we hear pandered today in the name of religion. It is when we loose sight of God's great purposes and plans for the salvation and liberation for the whole of creation, that we become self-absorbed and self-preoccupied. Instead of faith as a journey through our own inwardness until we come to the place where God meets us, it can become a journey into our own inwardness that dead ends on ourselves.

Mary can teach us how to praise God and enjoy God forever, even in the midst of adversity. She reminds us that God has great and sweeping plans, and our destiny is to become linked with

God's destiny for us and for the world. The song of this simple peasant girl echoes down the hallways of history and rings in our souls with liberating joy. We who bear the image of the invisible God belong to history, God's history, which is moving our history in the direction of God's future. Truly, God's salvation will have come to us when, with Mary, we can sing with full hearts, "My soul magnifies the Lord, and my spirit rejoices in God my Savior..."

Chapter 6: Study Aids

Note to the Leader: If you can get a copy of Albrecht Durer's "The Visitation," have it displayed as the group members arrive.

1. Elizabeth greeted Mary saying, "Blessed are you among women and blessed is the fruit of your womb." Where have we heard that before? (In the Hail Mary said by Catholics)

Hail Mary, full of grace,
the Lord is with thee;
Blessed are thou among women,
And blessed is he fruit of thy womb, Jesus."

2. Mary's response to Elizabeth's greeting is what the Church calls the Magnificat (Luke 1:46-55). Let's read it together. What strikes you as you hear this familiar canticle?

3. While Elizabeth praises Mary, Mary praises God. Mary rejoices, not in what she will do or accomplish but, in what God will do and accomplish in her and through her son. Let's examine what that will be. The Magnificat appears to speak of three revolutions that will take place: 1)a moral revolution (vs. 51), 2) a social revolution (vs. 52), and 3) an economic revolution (vs. 53).

A PROTESTANT DISCOVERS MARY

Any surprises here? Do we think at all in terms of revolutions when we consider our faith?

4. The author writes, "What God will accomplish through Mary's son will overthrow the very foundations of the world as it has been ordered by humanity. God will reorder the world according to justice, mercy, and peace. It will be a new order of life in God's Kingdom." How does this claim make you feel?

5. In Luke's version of the Sermon on the Mount, Jesus comes blessing the poor, the hungry, the downtrodden and the persecuted (Lk. 6:20-22). (Review the author's comment on these verses.) What is your response to these teachings of Jesus?

6. Jesus not only pronounced blessings, he also spoke woes. Let's read Luke 6:24-26 together. What is your response to these woes?

7. The author mentions God's "Preferential option for the poor." (Review author's comments.) Does this preferential option make sense or does it surprise you? Why?

8. The author writes, "Yes, dear Mary's blessing is not a purely personal one. She has a role in God's plan for the destiny of God's people, because Mary has conceived in her body the long awaited Messiah who will be the glory of Israel." Does this larger sweep of God's plan and purpose for God's blessings become for us instead a personal benefit and comfort?

9. How do you respond to the author's observation, "The tendency is so pervasive in our culture that we often confuse our own comfort, that has been grasped by our own hand, with God's blessing?"

10 Join with me as we close this session by saying together a Sending Forth numbered 1, in Part II of this study book.

CHAPTER 7
THE OBEDIENCE OF JOSEPH

"When Joseph woke from sleep, he did as the angel of the Lord commanded him;
he took his wife, but knew her not until she had borne a son;
and he called his name Jesus."
(Matthew 1:24-25)

In the ecumenical three year lectionary cycle, we read the Gospel of Matthew's nativity story every third year. The other two years we read Luke's account. Only Matthew and Luke give us accounts of Jesus' birth. Mark and John begin their gospel reports with Jesus' baptism. Matthew and Luke, in their birth stories, agree on the main points: that Jesus was born in Bethlehem, that his mother was the Virgin Mary, that his father (legally) was Joseph, and that Jesus' birth was the work of the Holy Spirit of God. Yet, Matthew and Luke diverge in numerous details and emphases. When we turn to Matthew's account of the birth of Jesus our Lord, we are struck very quickly with one overriding and remarkable difference from Luke's account.

A PROTESTANT DISCOVERS MARY

While Luke focuses upon Mary, Matthew presents the nativity from the perspective of Joseph. Therefore, it should be helpful to look at Mary and the story of Jesus' birth through the eyes and experience of Joseph. In this chapter, I want to look at Mary from the way Joseph, her betrothed, experienced the events surrounding the birth of Jesus.

My purpose is still the same, however. It is to help Protestant Christians discover Mary in both Scripture and Tradition. Mary is still the outstanding female Christian role model in the New Testament, and the New Testament is very short on female role models. Mary, of course, is also a wonderful model for *all* Christians. After Mary graciously said 'Yes' to God's plan, many problems remained. Would Joseph stand by her? In first century Israel, the young mother Mary would need a husband's protection. It would be very easy for Joseph to abandon her to a lonely humiliation. Worse still, Joseph could bring charges of adultery against Mary that would lead to her public humiliation. They could even result in her death by stoning.

As we read Matthew's narrative of the birth of Jesus, we find a certain kinship with Joseph. The response of us moderns is to look with deep skepticism upon the idea of a virgin becoming pregnant. What was a stumbling block for Joseph is also a stumbling block for us. In Joseph's place, we too would think it reasonable to divorce her quietly. In fact, some of us who may be carrying a good load of hostility in our spirits may even choose to divorce not so quietly. Some people always feel compelled to get even. Don't just get mad; get even! Everything becomes personal; every slight or perceived injury is confronted emotionally. Some folks deal with the day-to-day boredom in their lives by stoking their anger every chance they get.

Ask yourself these questions: How would I have played the part of Joseph in this drama? How would I have acted? How gracious of a person can I be when the chips are down? Some people become very self-destructive under pressure. When the pressure mounts, they seem compelled to do many of the things that will only hurt and few of the things that will help. Their reactions under pressure tell the lie on their actions the rest of the time. You could say it this way: Perhaps the best indicator of the work of God's grace in our lives is not so much how we act as how we *re*act.

Yes, we sense a kinship with Joseph's initial reaction to the news concerning the pregnancy of Mary his betrothed. I suspect we feel a bit in foreign territory, however, when we sense how Joseph behaved under the terrible humiliation that his wife was with child, and he was not the father. Before exploring Joseph's reaction in more detail, I believe the scripture cited at the head of this chapter presents us with certain difficulties regarding betrothal and marriage. If we are going to understand what Mary and Joseph faced, we need to understand these ancient cultural customs. Understanding these first century Jewish customs surrounding betrothal will illuminate Joseph's actual situation regarding Mary and the choices he faced.

When the New Testament reported Mary was betrothed to Joseph, we often understand that to mean about the same as our practice of engagement. However, that is not at all the case. In the modern world, engagement represents the serious commitment of a couple to develop a bonding relationship they hope will issue in marriage. Now if the relationship does not develop into a workable one that trusts, cares, and bonds, and that lays the foundation for marriage, then the engagement is wisely broken off. In this sense, it is very true to say that engagements are made to be broken, because they end either in separation or in marriage. It is never appropriate to treat a broken engagement as a failure. Yet, I know that is our tendency. Our initial reaction to a broken engagement is to see it as a failure. We put unhealthy pressure on couples to allow the momentum of engagements sweep them into unhappy marriages. In light of current divorce rates, I believe more engagements *should* be broken. It often happens that during the engagement, when a couple begins the more personal discovery of each other, they do not then assess whether the mutual discovery makes them good candidates or poor candidates for marriage. Blessed are those couples who have the courage to face the realization that their relationship has limited hope for lifetime bonding. After all, many persons are either not ready for or not mature enough for the mutual demands of marriage and lifelong bonding. Love is not enough!

Therefore, our modern practice of engagement is not an equivalent to betrothal. What then was the marriage situation that Joseph and Mary faced? At the point in time of the text cited above from Matthew 1, Joseph and Mary were in the latter stage of the first step in a two step marriage procedure. This first step was the formalized betrothal of a man and a woman based on a formal exchange of consent before witnesses. The betrothal was based on a written marriage contract and marked—get this!—the beginning of the transfer of a girl from her father's power and protection to her husband's power and protection. This usually occurred between the age of twelve and thirteen for first century Jewish brides. This would be at the onset of puberty. During the betrothal period, in which the couple was already considered husband and wife, the woman remained in her parent's home for one year. If anything existed which could annul the marriage contract, it was to be discovered during this one year period.

A betrothal could only end in three possible ways. The woman could become a widow, if the man died. Betrothal could end in a divorce, if either party (usually the man) discovered anything displeasing to him or her. The third way betrothal could end was with the charge of adultery. The person charged with adultery was formally charged by the spouse and put on trial. Since adultery was much harder to prove in a man than in a woman, generally only the woman suffered such charges. If the judgment of adultery were found against the wife, she typically would be stoned to death. So Mary, this thirteen or fourteen year old girl, could have been stoned to death, if Joseph had decided to make an issue out of Mary's pregnancy and bring formal charges against her.

Only after the one year betrothal period was ended, did the husband take his wife home with him. Only then did the married couple share board and bed. Now according to Matthew's Gospel, Mary and Joseph were in the one year betrothal period when Mary became pregnant. Joseph had not yet taken Mary home with him. Upon learning that Mary was with child, Joseph may have readily assumed Mary's condition to be the result of rape by a Roman soldier or the like. After all, Mary had recently made an extended visit to her relatives Elizabeth and Zechariah in the hill country of Judea. Who knows what may have happened on the journey or while Mary was there?

Joseph, Matthew reports, "being a just man and unwilling to put her to shame, resolved to divorce her quietly" (Matthew 1:19). Oh to God, that more divorces were quiet ones. In this brief verse, we learn much about the character of Joseph. He was a conscientious follower of God's law; yet, he did not wish to charge Mary with adultery and put her to public shame. Such a trial, of course, could issue in the death sentence as well. Joseph is holding a very strong hand, with all the trump cards. While poor Mary is exposed and totally vulnerable. She is in constant jeopardy because of her obedience to the word of God. As bystanders, we may logically conclude Mary's fate is in Joseph's hands. However, as people of faith we know Mary is in God's hands.

A PROTESTANT DISCOVERS MARY

Joseph, as a man of compassion, does not turn Mary into his enemy. He does not seek to hurt her back, as he himself obviously feels gravely injured. Instead, Joseph chooses the kinder, gentler, more gracious way, seeking to avoid any further hurts to anyone. Joseph chooses to divorce Mary quietly on some lesser charge than adultery. That would avoid a capital charge and put this whole traumatic episode quickly behind him. I am always amazed how some folks just won't let go of their pain. They insist on dragging yesterday's pain into all of their tomorrows. They allow hurts from the past to keep right on hurting them, over and over again. Not so, with the gentle spirited Joseph.

Are we not touched by the gentle, loving, spirit of Joseph? As surely as God must have prepared Mary for her special calling; so too must Joseph have been especially prepared to be Mary's husband. It would be of no use for Mary to tell Joseph that her child was conceived by the Holy Spirit. How could Joseph possibly believe that Mary had remained faithful to her betrothal vows? I mean, who would believe it? Only God can reach Joseph's wounded heart and heal his awful pain and bitter disappointment. Sometimes when we are wrapped in the mantle of our deep disappoints and pain, only God can finally reach us, and heal us, and set us free. During a night of troubled sleep, after Joseph had already resolved to divorce Mary quietly, God visited Joseph with an angel and spoke to him in a dream:

Joseph, son of David, do not fear to take Mary your wife, for that which is conceived in her is of the Holy Spirit; she shall bear a son, and you shall call his name Jesus, for he will save his people from their sins. (Matthew 1:20-21)

The next morning Joseph awoke from his night of troubled rest. Joseph struggled with the meaning of the heavenly visitation. Was it all only a dream? Was it just wishful thinking? Had the strange and unbelievable report by Mary unsettled Joseph? Could

God be wonderfully at work sending the promised Messiah of Israel in Mary's child? Had all this only confused his mind? A lesser person than Joseph would have found it easy to dismiss the night time visitation of the heavenly messenger, just as a lesser person than Mary would have found it easy to dismiss her own heavenly visitation. Joseph easily could have followed through on his earlier and quite generous resolve to divorce Mary quietly on a charge that he found something about her displeasing to him. 'After all', he could have reasoned, 'to divorce Mary quietly on a lesser charge is more than fair. What more can be expected of a man?' Surely, no one else could or would believe their story about God's Messiah. The town gossips—and every town and every church has them—would quickly spread their own versions of Mary's condition. Boy, the halls would be ringing after church that Sunday!

Yes, if Joseph takes Mary home with him to complete the second stage of marriage, he will protect Mary—but only somewhat. If Joseph obeys the heavenly visitation, he will claim the child to be his own, give the child a name, and take legal responsibility for the child. If he does this, as Matthew's Gospel seeks to make clear, Joseph will establish his paternity and Jesus may then trace his lineage through Joseph as a son of David. For in those ancient times, a legal dictum stated clearly the principle for establishing paternity: "If a man says, 'This is my son,' he is to be believed." For the ancients, paternity was defined in legal rather than in natural terms. The crucial point in those times was legal recognition, not biological descent.

Of course, such a claim of paternity for a child conceived out of wedlock would not be morally acceptable, since Joseph would be claiming that he violated the young virgin himself. Yet, it would be much better than to label Mary an adulterous woman and publicly humiliate her. However to protect Mary, it means that Joseph must face the community as a dishonored man married to a dishonored woman. He can only protect Mary at great costs to himself. Here Joseph becomes for us a model of humble obedience to God.

> *When Joseph woke from sleep, he did as the angel of the Lord commanded him; he took his wife, but knew her not until she had borne a son; and he called his name Jesus.* (Matthew 1:24-25)

Joseph "did as the angel of the Lord commanded him; he took [Mary] his wife [home with him]." The second and final step in marriage was now reached. By taking his betrothed wife into his own home, Joseph consummated the marriage. Joseph has now acknowledged the unborn child legally to be his own. Oh, that each of us, in the day of our visitation, may have the quiet courage of Joseph. Can we become as free as Joseph to do not only what is 'just,' but what is gracious and what is merciful? Joseph, with heaps of pride and self-righteousness, could have indignantly done the 'only fair and right thing.' Why should Mary's shame and pain become his own? 'If it is the work of God, let God do the work some other way.' Now, we've never said that before have we? If God wants it done, let somebody else do it. Why me? Why not someone else?

Yes Joseph, in his gracious reaction to Mary's plight, does not do the 'honorable' thing, which would have been to divorce her quietly. Joseph, instead, takes upon himself *dis*honor. He takes upon himself innocent and unwarranted pain and humiliation. Both of which Joseph could easily have avoided. Joseph says 'Yes' to God even when it means saying 'No' to himself. How much grace will we need in our lives in order for us to be as free as the gentle and obedient Joseph? How can we become as gracious as Joseph when we too are deeply hurt and sorely tried? Joseph had one great and shattering demand placed upon his life. He was able to rise to the occasion and meet that demand graciously (i.e., with grace).

May we embrace the advent of God in our lives, and so grow in grace, that each of us will be spiritually prepared for the hour of our visitation, when we like Joseph are faced with a shattering demand upon our lives. I say God bless Joseph!

Chapter 7: Study Aids

Note to the Leader: If you can find a copy of any picture showing Joseph, have it displayed as the group members arrive.
1. The Bible reports Mary and Joseph were betrothed. Betrothal is sometimes said to be like engagement. But this is not the case. (Review the book section of Mary and Joseph's marriage situation.) How does being betrothed differ from being engaged?
2. Betrothal could end in 3 ways. (See text.) Joseph chooses, what he believes is the more just way, to divorce Mary. Joseph "being a just man and unwilling to put her to shame, resolved to divorce her quietly" (Mt. 1:19). What do we learn about the character of Joseph from this decision?
3. The gracious spirit of Joseph is to put this whole thing behind him quietly. The author writes, "Instead Joseph chooses the kinder, gentler, more gracious way, seeking to avoid any further hurt to anyone." When a marriage fails and divorce happens, it is generally a painful experience. If only they happened quietly! We have all seen some very noisy, mean-spirited, even nasty divorces, haven't we? What feeds that bitterness?

4. Why so some people refuse to let go of their pain? "They insist on dragging yesterday's pain into all of their tomorrows."

5. The author writes, "Only God can reach Joseph's wounded heart and heal his awful pain and bitter disappointment." Isn't that where our healing lies? How do we allow God to heal our wounded spirits?

6. The author writes, "Oh, that each of us, in the day of our visitation, my have the quiet courage of Joseph. Can we become as free as Joseph and not rationalize our choices because they are 'just,' and instead do what is gracious and merciful?" Is it not easier to fall back on being just, rather than being gracious? Can we think of examples of being just rather than gracious?

7. Instead of doing the honorable thing to divorce Mary quietly, Joseph takes upon himself *dis*honor. How hard do you think that would be?

8. How can we become as gracious as Joseph when we are deeply hurt and sorely tried?

9. As we hear again this story, it sounds as though Mary's fate is in Joseph's hands. However, faith assures us this is not the case, doesn't it? Where does Mary's fate lie? How can we remember that our fate is in God's hands in the midst of life's crises?

10. Join with me as we close this session by reading responsively a Sending Forth numbered 4, in Part II of this study book.

Note to Leader: Ask the members to bring their Bibles with them next week, because we will be examining Mary in the biblical text outside of the nativity stories.

CHAPTER 8
MARY IN THE LIFE AND MINISTRY OF JESUS

In the previous chapters, focus has been upon the infancy narratives in Luke and Matthew. The annunciation, Mary's visit to Elizabeth with its Magnificat, the angel's visit to Joseph, the birth of Jesus in Bethlehem, and the flight of the holy family into Egypt are the most familiar traditions concerning Mary, the Mother of Jesus. Now we turn our attention to the place of Mary in the life and ministry of Jesus after the holy family was settled in Nazareth? How do the four Gospel writers present Mary during that period? Each of the writers presents his own unique approach to the Christian tradition and Mary's place in it. Just as each of the Gospel writers presents his own portrait of Jesus. Likewise, we will see diversity in the way they picture Mary.

Each of the four Gospels is a unique composition with special meaning for a particular community or audience of Christian disciples within the Church at large. These diverse Gospel portraits express the one gospel of Jesus Christ. It is believed, for example, that the Gospel of Mark was the first to be written of the four Gospels we now have in our Bibles. Both Matthew and Luke made use of Mark as a source for their Gospels. John's Gospel was written last among the four Gospels, perhaps reaching its final written form between 90 and 100 CE according to Raymond Brown.[18] John deliberately composed a Gospel that is highly symbolic and theological. Therefore, John's Gospel is in a class separate from the other three Gospels. Mark, Matthew, and Luke with their common view point are called *synoptic* Gospels, because they all follow the same basic synopsis of Jesus' ministry as set forth by Mark. There is not a great deal about Mary in these synoptic Gospels apart from the nativity narratives in Matthew and Luke. However, there is enough to ensure Mary's rightful place in the sacred memory of the Church. We will examine the tradition of Mary in each of the four Gospels with a focus on how Mary is presented during the ministry of Jesus.[19]

The Gospel of Mark

Mark is believed to be the earliest of the four Gospels. It was written around 50-55 CE, some twenty years after the resurrection of Jesus. It has remarkably little to say about Mary. Mark presents no birth narrative, but instead begins his account of the gospel with the baptism of Jesus at about thirty years of age. Joseph is not mentioned at all. Mary appears in only one incident in Jesus' ministry in Mark's Gospel. Jesus was accused of overworking and acting crazy or like a person possessed. Mary along with Jesus' brothers came for him, perhaps hoping to take him home away from public censure. They arrived at the house where Jesus was teaching, and they sent in a message asking Jesus to come out to them. The disciples reported to Jesus, "Look, your mother and brothers are outside, and they want you" (Mark 3:32). Jesus "looked over the people sitting around him" and replied to the messenger, "Look! Here are my mother and my brothers! Whoever does the will of God is my bother, my sister, and my mother" (Mark 3:35). As we shall see later, both Matthew and Luke softened this whole event including Jesus' words.

Mary is mentioned but does not appear in one other incident in Mark's account of the gospel. After establishing a successful ministry in the region around Lake Galilee, Jesus returned to his hometown of Nazareth where he had grown up. However, the local people took offence at him, so that he "could do no mighty work there." They questioned saying, "Isn't he the carpenter, the son of Mary, and brother of James, Joses, Judas, and Simon? Aren't his sisters living here?" (Mark 6:3). This mention of Mary along with brothers and sisters of Jesus is very important. First, it identifies Jesus with his mother with no mention of Joseph. Second, this historical reference to Jesus' family lends strong support to the Protestant view that Jesus had brothers and sisters who were children of Mary. Yet as we can see in both of Mark's references to Mary the mother of Jesus, he is rather negative in his treatment of Mary. Mary is seen only as the biological mother of Jesus and nothing more. She is not a member of the kingdom family. Matthew and Luke will alter Mark's view of Mary, as we shall see.

Mark insists that a blood relationship to Jesus is not important. Only a spiritual relationship to Jesus is what matters. Mark, the earliest Gospel writer, shows a general lack of interest in Jesus' historical roots and therefore in Mary as well. Mark concentrates on Christian discipleship as a matter of faith. The Church is made up of the spiritual brothers and sisters of Jesus. This lack of interest by Mark in Jesus' natural family and therefore in Mary is noted by Catholic writers. They see a preference for Mark's Gospel among Protestants that has influenced the Protestant estimation of Mary.

The Gospel of Matthew

The Christians for whom Matthew wrote his Gospel had strong Jewish traditions. They were concerned with the Jewish background of their faith in Christ. Matthew wrote an infancy narrative to preface his Gospel. It included a genealogy that traces Jesus' descent from the house of King David back to Father Abraham. Joseph, who gave legal descent for Jesus from King David, is dominant in his infancy narrative. Jesus is portrayed as the fulfillment of Israel's Law and Prophets. Jesus is the new Moses, a new law-giver. He is a new King David. He is born in Bethlehem, the city of David. He is born of a Jewish mother named Mary. For Matthew, Mary is more than a name and the biological mother of Jesus, as in Mark's Gospel. Mary is the virgin Mother of Israel, promised sign of the coming Messiah.

"Therefore the Lord himself will give you a sign. Behold, a young woman [or virgin] shall conceive and bear a son, and shall call his name Immanuel." (Isaiah 7:14)

God fulfills this divine promises to Israel, to Mary, and to the Church through the Holy Spirit.

Matthew also reports the incident recorded in Mark concerning Mary and Jesus' brothers.

He softens the whole episode. Jesus' family does not come to take charge of him, as in Mark. He simply reports that the family of Jesus came looking for him. The softened language in Matthew would be vital in a Christian Jewish memory about Mary, where James the "brother of the Lord" had become a prominent leader in the Jerusalem Church. Another incident, reported also in Mark, occurs when Jesus is visiting Nazareth and his family background and brothers and sisters are mentioned. Matthew does not say "Isn't he the carpenter, the son of Mary," as Mark had reported. Instead, he reports: "Isn't he the carpenter's son? Isn't Mary his mother...?" (Matthew 13:55) Matthew also, like Mark, adds the important reference to Jesus' family members.

"Aren't James, Joseph, Simon, and Judas his brothers? Aren't all his sisters living here?" (Matthew 13:55-56)

Note, unlike Mark, Jesus is not called the carpenter but rather the carpenter's son. This would mean that Joseph was the village carpenter and not Jesus. Of course, both Jesus and Joseph may have been carpenters, since a son often learned a trade from his father. At the cross, Matthew does not mention Mary's presence explicitly. However, he does mention a "Mary the mother of James and Joseph," whom it would appear was Jesus' mother since James and Joseph were the first sons mentioned earlier in Matthew 13:55. If that reference is to Mary the mother of Jesus, then it is highly significant because she is not mentioned first. Instead, Matthew gives prominence to Mary Magdalene:

"Among them were May Magdalene, Mary the mother of James and Joseph, and the mother of Zebedee's sons." (Matthew 27:56)

This would underscore that at this early stage of development in the Mary tradition, she is not yet so prominent a figure in the Church's memory.

The Gospel of Luke

Like Matthew, Luke also softened and expanded Mark's picture of Mary. Luke wrote primarily for a different audience that was less Jewish than with Matthew. It was more Greek in culture and interested less in Jewish origins than in a universal theology of discipleship. Mary is remembered in Luke's Gospel and in his sequel, the Acts of the Apostles, before and after Jesus' passion, death, and resurrection. Luke presents an elaborate infancy narrative that abounds in Old Testament influences. Luke links Jesus' birth with that of John the Baptist, who, according to Luke, was the son of Elizabeth and the old priest Zechariah.

Luke reports also the incident when Mary and Jesus' brothers came seeking him. Luke takes great care to distinguish the crowd from the disciples.

Jesus' mother and brothers came to him, but were unable to join him because of the crowd. Someone said to Jesus, "Your mother and brothers are standing outside and want to see you." Jesus said to them all, "My mother and brothers are those who hear the word of God and obey it." (Luke 8:19-21)

Jesus does not gesture, as in Mark, by pointing to the circle of disciples around him as those whoheard and kept the word of God. Thus, Luke does no separate Jesus' mother from his disciples but only from the crowd. After all, Luke has already reported that Mary has heard the word of God and kept it. In response to the angel Gabriel's message that God had chosen her to be the mother of the messiah, Mary answered, "Behold, I am the handmaid of the Lord; let it be to me according to your word" (Luke 1:38).

Luke also reports on this same theme an incident when a woman shouted out to Jesus a
blessing for his mother: "Blessed is the womb that bore you and the breast that gave you suck" (Luke 11:27). Jesus corrected the woman's blessing saying rather: "Blessed are they who hear the word of God and keep it." This, of course, is the exact beatitude, which Luke had already applied to Mary in his gospel. "And blessed is she who believed that there would be a fulfillment of what was spoken to her from the Lord" (Luke 1:45). The point of Jesus' reply to the woman who cried out the blessing, according to Luke, is that Mary is blessed not simply because of her motherhood but because of her response of faith and obedience upon hearing the word of God.

Mary is not excluded from the disciples by Luke. Although Mary is never listed among the disciples in Luke, Mary is portrayed by him as the first disciple. "Luke remembers Mary as the servant of God, filled with the Holy Spirit, full of faith, spreader o f the word, joyful mother of the Lord."[20] She personifies service to God. Later, in the Acts of the Apostles, Luke will place Mary with the disciples in the Jerusalem community of the post-resurrection church.

They all joined together in a group to pray frequently, together with the women, and Mary the mother of Jesus, and his brothers. (Acts 1:14)

It is important to note here that only Mary is singled out by name from among "the women." This is a marked development from Matthew, where, at the cross, he mentions Mary only after Mary Magdalene. Then she is not called "the Mother of Jesus," but rather "Mary the Mother of James and Joseph."

Luke also presents a genealogy of Jesus. He places it after the infancy narratives and just before the public ministry of Jesus. In keeping with Luke's gentile Greek audience, Jesus is portrayed as the savior of all peoples with his genealogy traced back to Adam. You recall that in Matthew Jesus' genealogy was traced back to Abraham, which served Jewish interests. Luke, alone, reports the presentation of Jesus in the temple by Joseph and Mary when the parents are required to make a redemption sacrifice for their newborn. This would have occurred following Mary's time of purification, after the birth of her son. Jesus would have been about six weeks old. Luke reports that a prophet named Simeon greeted the holy family at the Jerusalem Temple in the Court of the Women. He took the child in his arms and spoke of this new revelation "to the Gentiles."

Now, Lord, you have kept your promise, and you may let your servant go in peace. For with my own eyes I have seen your salvation, which you have made ready in the presence of all peoples: A light to reveal your way to the Gentiles, and to give glory to your people Israel. (Luke 2:29-32)

Luke also reports the same incident at Nazareth reported by Mark and Matthew, with a reference not to Mary but to Joseph. "Is not this the son of Joseph?" the people asked. He does not mention the brothers and sisters associated with this episode, as in Mark and Matthew. Unique to Luke (2:41-52) is the account of Jesus' visit to the temple with his family at age twelve. When his family left Jerusalem following the temple festival to return home to Nazareth, Jesus had stayed behind without the knowledge of his parents. Mary and Joseph discovered that Jesus was not among the caravan of pilgrims and searched for the boy Jesus. Then "on the third day" they find him in the temple confounding and amazing the teachers of the Law. Jesus then returned home in obedience to his parents.

Following the passion, death and resurrection of Jesus, Luke, in his sequel, again places Mary in Jerusalem among the disciples. There she is mentioned at a prayer meeting of the young church, along with the Lord's brothers. "All these with one accord devoted themselves to prayer, together with the women and Mary the mother of Jesus, and with his brothers" (Acts 1:14). Notice that Mary the Mother of Jesus is singled out for mention from among the women. This indicates that by the time Acts was written Mary's place in the sacred tradition has continued to develop so that her place is now important enough for her to be singularly mentioned as an important personage within the early church.

The Gospel of John

Like Matthew and Luke, John moves backward from the passion of Jesus, but not to the infancy of Jesus. He begins his

Gospel with the creation. Jesus is pictured as the divine word ("*logos*") that fulfills God's promise, not just to Israel but also the promise of God for all creation. John presents no birth narrative. After his prologue about the creation (1:1-18), John skips to the baptism of Jesus by John the Baptist. John's focus is on the eternal divinity of Jesus. Yet a characteristic of John's Gospel is his knowledge of detail about things Jewish and the geographical locations in Jesus' ministry. His gospel falls into three parts: the prologue (chapter 1), the "Book of Signs" (chapters 2-12), and the passion narrative (13f). In both the second and third parts, Mary is singled out in a particular episode.

In the second part of the Gospel of John (the 'Book of Signs'), Mary plays a key role in the first sign at Cana in The Galilee (John 2:1-12). In that miraculous sign, Jesus changed water into wine at a marriage feast. There Mary is called the Mother of Jesus. Mary initiates the action after noticing that the wine had been depleted. Why she felt this to be a concern of hers is uncertain. Perhaps Jesus' arrival with twelve disciples had helped to exhaust the supply. Mary appeals to Jesus to remedy the matter. Jesus, however, resists, "You must not tell me what to do woman. My time has not yet come "(Jn. 2:2). Nevertheless, Mary persists, saying to the servants: "Do whatever he tells you"(Jn. 2:5). Jesus then turned the water into wine. The meaning of the sign is to be seen in the details regarding the stone jars that were used for the Jewish rites of purification, the water becoming wine, and the abundance of wine produced. The result of this sign was that Jesus' disciples believed in him.

Walter Brennan summarizes contemporary interpreters of this first sign.

Therefore, if we look at the details, we see that the great biblical messianic banquet, an Old Testament familiar theme, is taking place. There will be a new wine and a new gift of the spirit, which will make the believers drunk with joy. The old temple rituals will fall away before the new templ3e, Jesus. The officials and non-believing Jews will not understand. Only servants of the banquet will know where the wine comes from as the final "hour" of the Lord begins.[21]

Mary, in the Gospel of John, is presented as the special mother, who like Eve is at the beginning and has a special role in getting the process started. She is the woman of the new creation. Jesus' brothers, however, are presented by John as unbelievers. "For even his brothers did not believe in him" (John 7:5). It is only after the resurrection that James, the Lord's brother, becomes a leader in the Jerusalem church. In the passion narrative, which is the third part of John's Gospel, Mary is again presented. This time she is among those who are at the foot of the cross. In fact, Jesus speaks to her directly from the cross, telling her to take 'the beloved disciple' for her son. To the beloved disciple, Jesus instructs him to take Mary for his mother.

When Jesus saw his mother, and the disciple whom he loved standing near, he said to his mother, 'Woman, behold, your son!' Then he said to the disciple, 'Behold, your mother!' And from that hour the disciple took her to his own home.   (John 19: 26-27)

Would this suggest that because Jesus' brothers did not yet believe in him, Jesus wanted to protect his mother by putting her into the care of one of his disciples? According to custom, Mary should have been in the care of her own sons.

Therefore, in John's Gospel, Mary plays a greater role in the tradition than we find in the earlier synoptic Gospels. It appears already in the tradition that there is a development visible in the Mary tradition. From Mark, where Mary is nearly non-existent except for one rather disparaging episode and in one other brief mention by name, Mary plays a prominent role in a number of episodes in John's Gospel. Now Mary is "mother of Jesus," "the woman," and "mother of the beloved disciple." Such titles are the early beginnings for subsequent theological development, just as were the titles for Jesus.

The Church's sacred memory of Mary, the Mother of Jesus, appears to have developed rapidly. Even during the time of the writing of the four Gospels, we see a development in the Tradition. After a rather negative assessment of Mary in Mark's Gospel, Mary begins to emerge as a disciple of Jesus in Luke and Matthew, and she is pictured by John as a significant influence in Jesus' ministry. Therefore, it is safe to say that, even without the nativity narratives in Matthew and Luke, Mary the mother of Jesus would be enshrined in the Christian tradition on the basis of what else the Gospel writers said of her. This is particularly true in the case of both Luke and John.

CHAPTER 8: STUDY AIDS

1. In this chapter, we will examine how the four Gospel writers portray Mary in the life and ministry of Jesus. (Review background to the nature of the four Gospels in the text.) Are there any questions, or comments? Any surprises?
2. **MARK:** He has no birth story. Mary appears in only one incident (Mk. 3:31-35). (Read together.) What is your impression of Mark's portrayal of Mary?
3. Mark mentions Mary in one other incident though she does not appear (Mk. 6:1-6). (Read together.) Note vs. 4 includes "among his own kin, and in his own house." It appears Jesus includes his own relatives and family in this indictment. (Note: Matthew keeps "in his own house," while Luke (4:24) drops the harsh phrase, reporting only "in his own country.") In Mark's account, what is Jesus saying about his family, including Mary?
4. **MATTHEW:** (See introduction to Matthew's Gospel in the text.) "Isn't he the carpenter's son? Isn't Mary his mother?" (Mt. 13:55) Notice, it is not "the carpenter" but the "carpenter's son." At the cross (Mt. 27:55-56), Mary is not made prominent.

She is named after Mary Magdalene and then only vaguely as "Mary the mother of James and Joseph." This is no doubt Mary the Mother of Jesus, since the two sons named are the same names of her two sons mentioned first in the earlier passage (vs. 13:55). Why not "Mary the Mother of Jesus?" What does this say about Mary?

5. **LUKE:** (See introduction to Luke's Gospel in the text.) Luke gives the most elaborate birth story. He softens and expands Mark's account of Mary. This suggests the Tradition regarding Mary is already developing. In Luke 11:27, note how Jesus responds to the shouted blessing of his mother. It is not about biology as in Mark. It is now about discipleship. Jesus' response reflects the blessing Luke has already applied to Mary in 1:45. "And blessed is she who believed that there would be a fulfillment of what was spoken to her from the Lord." Luke appears to portray Mary as the first disciple, although she is not listed among the disciples, since she was not called by Jesus to be a disciple. Is Mary as the first disciple a reasonable portrayal?

6. Luke, in his sequel the Book of Acts, places Mary prominently with the disciples in Jerusalem among the disciples and other believers in the post-resurrection church (Acts 1:14). Note that Luke shows a marked development of the Mary Tradition even compared with Matthew. While at the cross, Matthew only eludes to Mary as the mother of James and Joseph. Luke, however, refers to Mary as the Mother of Jesus after the resurrection. How do you respond to this development of the Mary Tradition?

7. Luke alone tells the story of the boy Jesus in the Temple and how his parents searched for him. (Read together Lk. 3:44-54.) Verse 46 reports Jesus' parents found him "after three days" or "on the third day." That is a very important phrase, since you may recall, Jesus, was raised up "on the third day." Even when they

found Jesus, Mary does not fully understand. How does that reflect on the Mary Tradition?

8. **JOHN:** (See introduction to John in the text.) John traces Jesus back not to Abraham, as in Matthew, but to creation. (Read together Jn. 1:1-18, esp. note vs. 1-5, 9-14.) In the 'Book of Signs,' chapters 2-12, Mary plays a key role in the first sign at Cana in The Galilee (Jn. 2:1-12). Mary is a special Mother, like Eve is at the beginning. Mary is the new Eve and plays an important role in getting the process started. The result of that miracle at Cana was Jesus "manifested his glory; and his disciples believed in him" (vs. 11). This was a very important development, since his disciples now believed in him in a new way! Comments or questions?

9. Mary is seen as an initiator in Jesus' ministry, while his own brothers still do not believe in him (Jn. 7:5, "For even his brothers did not believe in him.") How does this role of Mary suggest development in the Mary Tradition?

10. At the cross, John reports a singularly unique event concerning Mary, who is prominent in that incident. From the cross (how important does that make it?), Mary is placed in the care of the disciple John. Now Mary is Mother of John. Custom would dictate Mary would have been cared for by her own sons. How does this reflect the growing importance of Mary in the Jerusalem Church?

Note: Close this session by reading the last paragraph of this chapter in the text.

CHAPTER 9
RELATIONSHIPS IN THE AGE OF EVE AND THE AGE OF MARY

We have been looking at Mary from a biblical point of view. Now I want to turn our subject and look at Mary from another perspective. We will look at Mary as a means to help us interpret certain biblical texts. In this chapter, we will apply to Mary a hermeneutic principle to reflect upon some problematic passages of scripture. By hermeneutic, which means "to interpret," we will develop from Mary an interpretive principle to help illuminate the meaning of certain biblical texts. Early in the history of the Church there developed the idea of Mary as the new or second Eve. Very much in the same way the apostle Paul referred to Jesus as the new or second Adam (Romans 5:12-21).

Among the early biblical interpreters who helped formulate this concept of Mary as a new Eve was Irenaeus, who stamped this idea on the mind of Christendom. He contrasted Mary's obedience with Eve's disobedience. Eve in her disobedience became "a cause of death to herself and to all mankind. So Mary...was obedient and became to herself and to the whole human race a cause of salvation."[22] He also wrote, the "knot of Eve's disobedience was untied by Mary's obedience."[23] Later Chrysostom, the fourth century church father and patriarch of Constantinople, would write, "a virgin [Eve] had cast us out from paradise, through a virgin [Mary] we have found eternal life."[24] Ambrose, a fourth century saint and bishop of Milan, wrote, "Come then Eve, now Mary, who brought us not only virginity but God."[25]

With this perspective of an Eve/Mary hermeneutic in mind, we may speak of two ages: the Age of Eve and the Age of Mary. Using then this Age of Eve/Age of Mary as our hermeneutical principle, we turn to some very problematical verses of scripture, passages that are difficult both to interpret and to reconcile with other passages. Which of the passages will trouble us reveals our biases. Some verses we would embrace, while others we would avoid. It is my hope to apply the Eve/Mary hermeneutic to these passages in a way that helps us interpret them within the framework of the biblical tradition. Such an approach, I suspect, will be a positive alternative to a 'picking and choosing' approach. First, let me cite the diverging texts.

Do you want to find support in the Bible for the view that men are dominant and women are subordinate? Here are texts that are understood to support you.

"Likewise you wives by submissive [or 'subject'] to your husband."
(I Peter 3:1)
"Let a woman learn in silence with all submissiveness."
(I Timothy 2:11)
"Yet woman will be saved through bearing children, if she continues in faith and love and holiness with modesty."
(I Timothy 2:15)
"Wives, be subject to your husbands, as to the Lord. For the husband is the head of the wife as Christ is the head of the

church." *(Colossians 3:18)*
"As the church is subject to Christ, so let wives also be subject in everything to their husbands." *(Ephesians 5:24)*
"For man ought not to cover his head, since he is in the image and glory of God, but woman is the glory of man." *(I Corinthians 11:7)*
"As in all the churches of the saints, the woman should keep silence in the churches, for they are not permitted to speak but should be subordinate as even the law says." *(I Corinthians 14:33-34)*
"But I want you to understand, that the head of every man is Christ, the head of a woman is her husband, and the head of Christ is God." *(I Corinthians 11:3)*
"For man was not made for woman, but woman for man. Neither was man created for woman, but woman for man." *(I Corinthians 11:8-9)*

Perhaps you do not like these verses. You would like to quote some other verses that give another perspective. The following verses, perhaps, will spark a little spirit among those who hold a different view. Do you want to find biblical support for the view that men and women are equal in Christ? Consider, then, these verses.

"Nevertheless in the Lord woman is not independent of man, nor man of woman." *(I Corinthians 11:11)*
"There is neither [the word is literally 'there can not be'] Jew nor Greek, there is neither slave nor free, there is neither male nor female. For you are all one in Christ Jesus." *(Galatians 3:28)*
"Be subject to one another out of reverence for Christ." *(Ephesians 5:21)*
"For just as the body is one and has many members, and all of the members, though many, are one body, so it is with Christ." *(I Corinthians 12:12)*

"For by one spirit, we were all baptized into one body, Jews or Greeks, slaves or free. And all were made to drink of one spirit."
(I Corinthians 12:13)
"For as many of you as were baptized into Christ have put on Christ... So through God you are all no longer a slave but a son, and if a son than an heir." (Galatians 3:27, 4:7)
"For the wife does not rule over her own body, but the husband does. Likewise, the husband does not rule over his own body, but the wife does." (I Corinthians 7:4)

The texts in this second list suggest mutuality and equality between woman and man. The above two groups of biblical texts prove only one thing. *The proof text approach to this subject is inadequate, because you can find biblical texts that support either of these views.* So the nature of life together in Christ, the relationship between woman and man, the understanding of marriage and the family in Christian homes cannot be ordered by quoting a series of proof texts. Though that has generally been the practice. Instead, all the biblical texts in both lists need to be understood and informed by the new order of life in Jesus Christ. This new order is a foretaste of how life shall be ordered in the Kingdom of God.

We may look at these clearly contradictory scriptures through the lens of the Eve/Mary principle. This hermeneutic can give us a method for understanding them and relating them. Eve represents the old order of rebellious and fallen humanity, what may be called the Age of Eve. While Mary represents the new order of life in Christ, what may be called the Age of Mary. The Age of Eve is characterized by woman after the stories of creation and the fall, as we find them in Genesis. Eve is disobedient to the word of God. Eve is shown in Genesis to be created for man as a "help mate" or "helper" (Genesis 2:18).

Reflecting this Age of Eve, much of the New Testament tradition of the subordination of women quotes or rests upon the story of Eve having been created from Adam's rib. Other texts rest upon the view of Eve as temptress, who counsels the 'innocent' Adam to fall into sin because of the seduction of the serpent. Jewish Law even prescribed such subordination of women. Paul refers to it in I Corinthians 14:34, "For they [women] are not permitted to speak, but should be subordinate, as even the law says." In Judaism, for example, the study of the scriptures and the practice of worship were totally the work of men. A twelve year old boy in ancient Judaism had more status before God and in society than his own mother. A twelve year old boy! Therefore, from the earliest times we find women severely circumscribed and limited.

Even in the Gentile world as early as the second century B.C.E., women's emancipation seems to have been a problem for men. Cato the Elder, in 195 B.C.E., predicted disaster should wives receive any more rights that would free them from a subordinated status to their husbands. Cato wrote:

Review all the laws with which your forefathers restrained their license and made them subject to their husbands; even with all these bonds you can scarcely control them. What of this? If you suffer them to seize these bonds one by one and wrench themselves free...do you think that you will be able to endure them: the moment they begin to be your equals, they will be your superiors.[26]

Therefore, Cato said men have to oppress women or else women would become better than men. They would be superior! That is a remarkable admission. Well, at least Cato was clear why he was oppressing women. He thought them to be the superior of the species. I suspect most oppression of other people is motivated out of some sense of fear of those who are being oppressed. The subordination of women physically and socially was spelled out by the Church theologically. Some of the Church

Fathers even went so far as to teach—and I think this will surprise most people—that for women to enter into the afterlife they first had to become men. This necessary transmutation occurred at the moment of death. Thus, women took on the image of God who was seen in grossly physical male terms. Only then were women seen fit to be with God in paradise. Women, in order to be saved, had to become men. Some of the Fathers of the Church actually taught that!

The Age of Eve characterizes the old order in which women are seen as inferior but necessary sex objects, human incubators, and domestic servants. It reminds me of a close friend of ours, a highly successful career woman with two children who is married and has what may be considered a better job than her husband—including making more money than he does. She casually mentioned, with tongue in cheek, that what she needed now was a good wife. The Age of Eve! Who is this person who happens to be a woman? Is she defined, confined, and restricted by her womanhood? Is she first a daughter of Eve, or is she first a daughter of the living God?

Fortunately, there is another age. A new age has dawned, the Age of Mary. It is an age, which characterizes the new order of life in Christ. In the Age of Mary, woman is designated as "chosen of God," "bearer of the promise of salvation," "partner with God in the redemption of the world." While Eve was defined by her physical creation and spiritual rebellion, Mary, the Mother of Jesus, is defined by God's choosing, God's promise, and her own great faith. No longer is woman simply Eve, the "Mother of all Living," as Genesis (3:20) described her. Woman is now Mary, faithful handmaiden of the Lord, woman of faith, partner of God, Mother of the Messiah, and Mother of the Church. The Age of Mary gives women a new status. Woman is no longer defined and limited by the stories of creation and the fall. She is now defined and set free by the story of redemption and faithfulness. Woman is no longer Eve, the helpmate of man. She is now Mary, the partner of God in the unfolding drama for the salvation of the world.

A remarkable story in the New Testament that illustrates this emerging new status of women in Christ is the story of Martha and Mary of Bethany. We all know it well. Mary and Martha and their brother Lazarus were good friends of Jesus. When Jesus was in the vicinity of Jerusalem, he would often stay with them in Bethany that lay about two miles east of Jerusalem, just over the crest of the Mount of Olives lying on its eastern slope. When Jesus did not cross the mountain and stay with these friends in Bethany, he often found shelter among the trees on the Mount of Olives along the bottom of its western slope in Gethsemane, opposite the holy Temple in Jerusalem.

One day while Jesus was visiting in Bethany at the home of his friends, he sat discussing with his disciples. With all those guests, someone had to provide for their hospitality including meals. Martha was out in the kitchen fretting over the preparation of a meal for so many. While Mary, her sister, had slipped out of the kitchen and was sitting at the feet of Jesus, listening to this big religious discussion going on among the men folk. Martha came out of the kitchen and said in desperation something to the effect, "Jesus, will you talk to Mary so she will come back in the kitchen and help me with the cooking as she is supposed to do?" How does Jesus respond to Martha's request? Does he scold Mary for her dereliction of the duty of hospitality? That was an almost sacred duty in ancient Israel. However, Jesus does not scold Mary and send her back into the kitchen. Instead, Jesus addresses Martha and not Mary,

Martha, Martha, you are anxious and troubled about many things. One thing is needful. Mary has chosen the good

*portion, which shall not be taken away from her.
(Luke10:41-42)*
Jesus does not side with the old order, the order of Eve. He does not send Mary hurrying back into the kitchen, as though only men need to deal with and handle the things of God. Jesus blesses Mary with a new status, one that honors her presence sitting among the disciples discussing the things of the Kingdom of God. Providing hospitality, which was an important obligation in ancient Israel, is subordinated to the dawning of the new age of the kingdom of God. Jesus enables women to choose what roles they will take. Vladimir Lossky, that brilliant interpreter of the theology of the Eastern Church, in his *The Mystical Theology of the Eastern Church*, marks the abolishment of the division between male and female to the virgin birth of Jesus. Lossky writes, "By his birth of the Virgin, He suppresses the division of human nature into male and female."[27] In this view, the human division between male and female has been overcome by the way Christ Jesus was born of the Virgin Mary without male/female procreation. By the incarnation of God in this manner, a new Adam is born into the world (Romans 5:12-21) and gives a new beginning to the human race, one that is not defined the old divisions. So now, all of us are united as one new person in Jesus Christ.

What do we say then about those New Testament passages of subordination? First, we can say that such passages represent the lingering shadows of the old Age of Eve, which characterized Jewish practice since well before the time of Christ and before the Age of Mary. Subordination of women was even prescribed in their Law.   Secondly, some of those verses need to be understood in light of other verses. This is an early Protestant principle of biblical interpretation. Let scripture interpret scripture. Here is just one example of the use of this biblical principle. In Ephesians 4:22 we read, "Wives be subject to your husband as to the Lord." What does that mean here for a woman to "be subject to" her husband? The clue comes one verse earlier, in verse 21, where we read, "Be subject to one another, out of reverence for Christ." Be "subject to" each other. That means males are subject to males; females are subject to other females; females are subject to males; and males are subject to females—a *mutual subjection* to one another as Christians. The kind of subjection wives are to have to their husbands is the same kind of subjection we all are to have towards each other, including the subjection of males to females, and husbands to wives.

Does that change our understanding of subjection? Subjection does not mean obedience, which is the relationship between parent and child as described in Ephesians 6:1: "Children, obey your parents in the Lord, for this is right." Then, and only then, in relation to children the writer speaks of obedience and not subjection. *Our relationship, in Christ, between adult and adult, whether male or female, is never one of subordination but one of mutual subjection.* The relationship between parent and child is one of obedience. Subjection means to subordinate one's self, just as some men are subordinate to other men and even to women. As Christians, we are freely to subordinate ourselves to each other, and so fulfill the law of love. The husband and wife relationship is further defined in Ephesians 5:25, where the husband's role is not self-assertion over his spouse but self-sacrifice. The husband and wife relationship among Christians is to be modeled after the relationship between Christ and his Church, and not after parent and child relationships.

This relationship between married partners is a uniquely beautiful relationship among all of the relationships of life. This marriage relationship is used as a symbol of the relationship between God and God's people. It runs throughout the Bible. The marriage analogy is implied in the very idea of covenant. The theme of covenant is itself a summary of the themes of the Bible. Hosea the prophet, in the eighth century before Christ, gives us a matchless picture of God as a loving and forgiving husband and Israel as an erring wife who has run away to become a prostitute. Yet, he still loves her! God's covenant love is not destroyed by Israel's unfaithfulness. In the last chapter of the New Testament, the Church is pictured as the bride of Christ.

The highest insight representing the new order of life in the Age of Mary, regarding the order of relationships between woman and man, is reached by Paul in Galatians. Here is the Age of Mary at its zenith, when all formerly assigned roles and human divisions are transcended in Jesus Christ. Paul writes, and I am giving a literal translation,

"There cannot be Jew or Greek. There cannot be slave or free. There cannot be male or female. For you are all one in Christ Jesus." (Galatians 3:26).

The fractured order of life in the Age of Eve has been superseded and restored by the new order of unity and mutuality in the Age of Mary.

Here is the heart of Christian marriage and the family—oneness in Jesus Christ. Here is not subordination but *mutual subjection*. There is no place in the Age of Mary for a heavy handed treatment of our brothers and sisters in Christ, even when we are married to one of them. The Age of Eve, with its limited view of woman in the design of God, has been superseded by the Age of Mary, in which all of us—male and female—are now defined by our rebirth more than by our birth. Our divine vocation, as declared in our baptism into Jesus Christ, supersedes all that defined and limited us in the old order of life. In the Age of Mary, we are all new creatures in Christ Jesus and have been set free for the new order of life in the Kingdom of God.

Chapter 9: Study Aids

1. In this session, we will be using a term that may be unfamiliar to some of us. It is the term hermeneutic and the form hermeneutical. In simple terms it means "to interpret" a text. The field of hermeneutics concerns the study of how to interpret a written text and is not limited to biblical texts. Are there any questions or comments about this term and its use?

2. The hermeneutical principle the author uses is Age of Eve/ Age of Mary. It goes back to the biblical idea of Mary as the new Eve. (See the paragraph in the chapter that deals with the concept of Mary as new Eve in the early Church Fathers. Read it together.) Are we familiar with the idea of Mary as the new Eve? Comments or questions?

3. Let's examine the list of biblical verses that support domination and subordination of women. (Read this list together from the chapter.) How are we to understand these biblical texts?

4. Let's examine the list of biblical verses that support equality of men and women in Christ. (Read this list together from the chapter.) Any surprises here?

5. The author claims that the two lists of biblical verses prove only one thing. "The proof text approach to this subject is inadequate, because you can find biblical texts that support either of these views." How familiar are we with a proof text approach to understanding the Bible? Have you seen it used in connection with other parts of the Bible?

6. Let's review how the author explains the Age of Eve/Age of Mary hermeneutical principle. (Read together the paragraphs that explain it.) Questions or comments about the hermeneutic the author is suggesting? Is it a reasonable, biblical hermeneutic?

7. Perhaps the best example when Jesus directly addressed the changing role of women is the story of Mary and Martha. Let's read it together in Luke 10:38-42. There is a tension in this story. How would you describe it?

8. The author writes, "Our relationship in Chris between adult and adult is never one of subordination but one of mutual subjection." What is meant by mutual subjection?

9. This has been a demanding chapter and session. Are than any comments or questions before we close?

CHAPTER 10
TITLES FOR MARY

Titles are the beginning of theology. We need only to look at the example of titles for Jesus to understand this. The Church's Christology is embodied in these titles from Rabbi to God Incarnate, so too in the Church's Mariology. Throughout the history of the Church's Tradition, many titles have been given to Mary. These titles range from the mundane to the profound, from Mother of Jesus to Mother of God. Perhaps it would be beneficial to the reader to have a list of some of the most recognized titles for Mary. Some of these titles will be preferred by Protestants who are not always sympathetic to Marian devotion, while others will be preferred by those who practice such piety. However, all are titles for Mary that have been used to designate her place in both faith and practice. While reviewing these titles for Mary, it would be helpful to heed the guidance of Vatican II in *Lumen Gentium*, "Let them rightly explain the offices and privileges of the Blessed Virgin which are always related to Christ, the source of all truth, sanctity, and piety."

With Vatican II, the Catholic Church has begun a reform of

Marian devotion to curb exaggeration and excess regarding the Virgin Mary and to emphasize the central role of Jesus Christ in salvation and mediation. This can be nothing but encouraging news to Protestant Christians who have objected to such excesses and to the accompanying diminished centrality of the role of Christ. A new opening for a more ecumenical spirit occurred in the Second Vatican Council when the Church resisted any expansion of Mary's roles and titles and instead sought to find a more biblical grounded tradition of Mary. This newer approach to Mary led the Council to place its statements about Mary within the Constitution of the Church rather than to publish a separate document on Mary. This ecumenical approach of the Council concerning Mary was expressed in a touching way by the Pope in the presentation of the final document *Lumen Gentium*. He said,

It is the first time, in fact, and saying it fills our souls with profound emotion, that an Ecumenical Council has presented such a vast synthesis of the Catholic doctrine regarding the place which the Blessed Mary occupies in the mystery of Christ and of the Church.

Protestant Christians can only be encouraged by the manner in which the Second Vatican Council in 1964 proclaimed its teaching regarding the memory of Mary.

Joined to Christ the Head, and in communion with all his saints, the faithful must in the first place reverence the memory "of the glorious ever Virgin Mary, Mother of God and of our Lord Jesus Christ." She is hailed as preeminent and as a wholly unique member of the Church, and as its type and outstanding model in faith and charity.[28]

How will this play among Protestants? Will we take a fresh look at the renewed picture of Mary and her place in our faith tradition? If the reforms of Marian devotion that we have called for as Protestants are now being addressed and even embraced by the Catholic Church, does that not require of us to look again at Mary and her place in the tradition with fresh eyes?

This renewal of Marian devotion is part of a larger reform in the Catholic Church that has begun to emphasize Scripture along side the Tradition. This new biblical emphasis can only be celebrated by Protestant Christians. It has led to the establishment of Catholic adult education centers in the post-Vatican Church. I recall, as a young pastor, arranging with a post-Vatican Catholic adult education center in Rockford, Illinois to offer a United Methodist sponsored course on the Sermon on the Mount taught by my supervisor and me. Members of the class included many Catholic laity and several nuns. Is that not Church reform, when Catholics and Protestants can sit together and study the Bible?

Efforts to achieve ecumenical perspective on Mary have led to further suggestions for reform by Catholics. Anthony Tambasco, a professor of theology at Georgetown University, has clearly characterized this new perspective on Mary. No longer is "Mary viewed as joined with Christ facing the Church in the work of redemption," instead she is viewed as "joined to the Church facing Christ and being redeemed by Christ who is the all-sufficient mediator of salvation."[29] This shift in perspective was expressed by Pope Paul VI at the close of Vatican II when he proclaimed Mary "Mother of the Church." This helpful title was well received generally, but it did not satisfy those who wanted an expansion of Mary's place and role in the Church's faith. Frederick Jelley, writing on the reappraisal of Mary's office of intercession, offered helpful guidelines to further this reform. "Mary and the saints do not hear the prayers and grant the favors; Christ has the unique role of mediator. One does not approach Mary because Christ is remote. Since God himself is merciful, Mary and the saints do not function to make God more favorable toward us. The saints are not relay stations. Mary does not substitute for Christ. Mary is a subordinate means of grace, but not the source. We are not unworthy to approach God directly ourselves."[30]

We Protestants can begin our own reform by taking a fresh look at the titles the Church has given to Mary through the centuries. Some of these titles are weighted with theologies that Protestants have found objectionable. Some are not. Some titles simply are not well understood by Protestant Christians. Therefore, we begin a fresh examination of the titles for Mary. The following suggestive list of titles for Mary is in no particular order and includes both biblical and dogmatic titles. Biblical titles are lifted out of the texts of the Bible, such as Handmaid of the Lord (Luke 1:16). While dogmatic titles emerge from doctrinal positions, such as Mother of God, which emerged from the doctrinal dispute regarding the two natures of Jesus Christ. Of course, there are many more titles for Mary than those listed here. Vatican II, in *Lumen Gentium*, styled Mary as Mother 16 different ways. Therefore, this list of titles for Mary is only a sampling of titles

Titles for Mary
Mary of Nazareth
Queen of Peace,
Handmaid of the Lord
Queen of Apostles
Blessed Mary
Queen of Heaven
Consort (Consortium)
Queen of the Universe
Virgin Mary
New Eve
Blessed Virgin Mary

A PROTESTANT DISCOVERS MARY

Bride of God
Holy Virgin
Spouse of God (or of Christ)
Holy Mother
Madonna
Mother of our Lord
Our Lady
Mother of Christ
Our Lady of Mercy
The Mother (or Our Mother)
Mediatress (Mediatrix)*
Mother of the Church
Co-redemptress (Co-redemptrix)*
Mother of God
Theotokos (God-Bearer)

The two titles marked with an asterisk (*) in the above list, perhaps more than any others, have caused confusion and have proven obstacles for many Protestants. Titles such as these that give Mary a special role in mediation and redemption have hindered Protestant Christians generally from giving proper place to Mary in their faith and in their churches. A number of titles in this list are not well understood because of a general neglect of Mary among Protestants. Some dogmatic titles that claim Mary shares with Christ in his saving work have served as obstacles to many Protestants. Such titles for Mary have been challenged as well by some in the Catholic Church and have been discouraged generally since Vatican II. These titles suggest or imply Mary has a conjoint role with Christ in the work of salvation as co-redeemer (Redemptress or Redemptrix) and co-mediator (Mediatress or Mediatrix). Many Protestants find objectionable such titles for Mary that claim or infer conjoint responsibility with Christ in his saving work. These titles have only served to engender misunderstanding and confusion among many Protestants about Mary's rightful place in the Church. They are real obstacles to any ecumenical perspective regarding Mary. Fortunately, Vatican II, and subsequently the Church generally, has sought to distance the Church from titles for Mary that suggest or imply that she shares in the work of Christ for our salvation.

Protestants need to appreciate what the Catholic Church achieved at Vatican II regarding Mary. At the Council, there was tremendous pressure to extend Marion devotion by giving greater definition and teaching authority for some form of a role for Mary as co-mediator or co-redeemer. This effort was both feverish and tension filled. However, this effort was clearly resisted by the Council as it sought to emphasize the singular role of Christ who brings salvation to all, including Mary. Even the title for Mary as Mediatress of all graces was neither defined nor declared by the Council. Marion devotion had to give way to a Marion theology with a renewed methodology and content. The Council rejected a separate document on Mary, while a sizable and vocal minority sought to include it. Instead, the Council created an abbreviated statement on Mary as a chapter in its document on the Church. Tambasco summarizes this action, "It said by its very location that theology of Mary needs to be inserted into the context of other theology and that Mary needs to be seen not simply next to Jesus in some qualified way in the work of redemption, but also within the Church as fully redeemed herself."[31]

In this brief chapter, I want to focus on only two of the above listed titles for Mary. These two titles are singled out for several reasons. They are centrally important titles with a very ancient pedigree; they are not generally well understood among Protestant Christians; and they are often dismissed out of hand. Unlike titles such as Mediatress, Cohort, and Co-Redemptress, which are rejected by many Protestants for solid theological reasons, the titles Mother of God and Theotokos are often rejected, I believe, more out of a misunderstanding of what these titles actually teach. Briefly then, I want to highlight what these two very important titles are saying about Mary and about the doctrine of Christ. With a better understanding of these two titles, I believe many Protestants will be able to embrace them.

Mother of God

This title has been called "the fundamental title"[32] for Mary in the Catholic Church. This widely used and very early title Mother of God is not well understood by many Protestants. I believe it would be more widely accepted, if it were more clearly *nuanced*. It is evident to all that this title for Mary is not found in the New Testament. However, that alone does not diminish it, any more than the fact that the term Trinity does not appear in the NT. Yet, the doctrine of the Trinity is a core belief of the Church. The key to appreciating this title is to understand how the title emerged in the teaching of the Church. The title Mother of God was given to Mary as a *corollary* to the ancient Church's Christology. The Church was embroiled in controversy for centuries as it tried to work out its understanding of the doctrine of Christ, its Christology. This title for Mary emerged as the Church defended Christianity and its doctrine of Christ against those who rejected the Incarnation of God in Jesus of Nazareth. The Church needed to clarify its doctrine of Christ and how it understood what it means that Christ was both human and divine.

At the Council of Chalcedon in 451,[33] the Church gave a more detailed analysis of the union and the distinction of the two natures in the one person of Jesus Christ. The title for Mary as Mother of God was already in use and was a kind of doctrinal litmus test. It was at the Council of Ephesus, twenty years earlier, that the title Mother of God (*Theotokos*) was formally used by the teaching authority of the Church. Now at Chalcedon, the Church insisted that God became "truly God and truly human." This Jesus who was the Christ was truly human, "like us in all things, except sin," and he was truly divine, "begotten before all ages of the Father according to the Godhead..." The fullness of Christ's humanity was defended, saying Christ was "born of the Virgin Mary, Mother of God (*Theotokos*), according to the humanity." For those untrained in theology, the controversy over the two natures doctrine may seem exaggerated and even unimportant. The Church, however, recognized that this issue was central to its understanding of the person and work of Jesus Christ. It was seeking to defend its doctrine of Christ against false doctrines (e.g. heresies) that are still with us today.

How shall we understand this business of the two natures of the one Jesus Christ? Perhaps it would be helpful in understanding the doctrine of the two natures to state what views of the nature of Christ the Church rejected. These false views of Christ Jesus that the doctrine of the two natures meant to avoid have been clearly stated by Robert Clyde Johnson,[34] in his masterful little book on Christ written for the laity quite a number of years ago. I simply mention them here, since Johnson stated them in a most succinct manner. There were basically three Christological heresies.

1. Jesus was "a Manlike God (but not really a man)" who was really a God pretending to be human and knew everything God knew. To this, the Church countered that Jesus was "truly human" and "like us in all things, except sin."

2. Jesus was "a Godlike Man (but not really a God)." He was only a godly man, an amazing teacher, and nothing more. To this, the Church countered that Jesus was "truly God," was "consubstantial with the Godhead" and "begotten before all ages of the Father according to the Godhead..."

3. Jesus was a "God/Man (but neither really God nor really man)" with some combination (blend or "confusion") of the divine and human natures that made him divided and alien from both our humanity and God's divinity.

This doctrine of the two natures of Jesus Christ, who was both divine and human, made it clear that the divine nature came from God through the Holy Spirit, while the human nature came from his Mother Mary. The "Symbol of Chalcedon," as the Council's statement is known, referred to the Virgin Mary, calling her the Mother of God (*Theotokos*), "…born of the Virgin Mary, the Mother of God (*Theotokos*), according to the humanity; one and the same Christ, Son, Lord, Only-begotten, to be acknowledged in two natures…" Karl Rahner, the eminent Catholic theologian, has been helpful in reminding us of this connection of the title Mother of God with this important core doctrine of the two natures. He writes that the divine motherhood "really concerns and has more to say about the union of two natures in the unity of the one person of the Word of God than about Mary herself."[35]

A carefully nuanced understanding of the doctrine of the incarnation of God the Son, second Person of the Holy Trinity, leads to the recognition that Mary's son is God the Son made flesh. Mary gave herself and her humanity soul and body, at God's choosing, to bear God into the world in human flesh. Therefore, Mary may rightfully be called the Mother of God *in that sense*. However, the title becomes misleading to the uninformed in that it may lead to the mistaken conclusion that the title Mother of God means. Mary is the Mother of the Godhead or Holy Trinity. Such a misunderstanding would place Mary above God the Holy Trinity. Mary is not Mother of God the Father or Mother of God the Holy Spirit. She is, none the less, Mother of the Incarnate God, God the Son, the Divine Word become human.

Theotokos (God-Bearer)

A title that carries a similar meaning to the title Mother of God, but without its inherent confusion, is the Greek title *Theotokos*. This title was, in fact, the exact term the Council of Chalcedon used in reference to Mary. The Symbol (or Decree) of Chalcedon declared that Jesus was "…born of the Virgin Mary, the *Theotokos*, according to the humanity…" The title *Theotokos* is highly esteemed in the Eastern (Orthodox) Church where Mary is given her proper place in both its tradition and its liturgy. '*Theotokos*' is a Greek term that is formed by combining two Greek words: '*Theo*', which is a form of the word '*Theos*' that means "God," and '*tokos*' that means "the *bearer* of a child" or "giving birth." '*Theotokos*' is rendered into English as the "God-Bearer." This title has been rendered in the Western Church as "Mother of God." A case may certainly be made for such a translation. However, it should be noted that the Greek word for mother (*metros*) was not used in the title for Mary at Chalcedon. The title given Mary was not *Theometros* but *Theotokos*. Therefore, the title given to Mary at Chalcedon was not precisely Mother of God but rather Bearer of God. Therefore, the Western translation of the title '*Theotokos*' as "Mother of God" is somewhat misleading, though understandably clear.

This distinction may appear rather minor on the surface, but, in fact, it may be quite substantial. Mary was not the source and did not generate the Second Person of the Trinity in her womb. Rather, the Holy Spirit "overshadowed" Mary so that she became "Mother of the incarnate Word of the eternal Father"[36] who grew in her blessed womb by the power of God's Spirit. It is God who generates and God who causes to grow. God begets the Son by the Holy Spirit and causes to grow in Mary's womb this unique person with two natures who is both "truly divine and truly human." Mary is a God's chosen vessel, which bears God's Son into human flesh. Because of this divine maternity, Mary has a place in our creeds and in our piety. The marvelous title *Theotokos* appears to avoid some of the confusion associated with the title Mother of God, while it still expresses Mary's unique and divinely chosen role in her divine maternity, as the woman who uniquely bears God into a human life in the world.

By giving her body to be the *Theotokos*, Mary also gives her DNA, her genes, her womb, her flesh, even her very soul, in order to "bear God" into human life and human history. God's nature and human nature are discretely united by God in the one person of Jesus Christ in Mary's virgin womb, so that the son she bore was also God's Son. The Church carefully defined and defended this doctrine of the two natures of Christ at the Council of Chalcedon in 451. Our Lord Jesus Christ was declared "perfect in Godhead and also perfect in manhood; truly God and truly human...born of the Virgin Mary, *Theotokos*, according to the humanity...Only-begotten, to be acknowledged in two natures..." Then follows the delightful formula that was meant to preserve and defend the doctrine of Christ having two natures which were "...*without confusion, without change, without division, without separation*..."[37]

Clearly, the Church declared that Jesus Christ's divine nature and human nature were not confused, mixed or blended together into one nature. They were "without change," so that the two natures remained intact at all times with each retaining the properties unique to each nature. They were also "without division," so that the divine nature remained fully divine while the human nature remained fully human united in the one person of Christ; the properties of each nature could not be divided between the two natures, so that the two natures were now somehow altered; and they could not be separated from each other, thus destroying the unique God given union, or from their origin in the Godhead and in humanity. In other words, each of the two natures was complete in itself; each nature retained at all times its own distinctive properties and operations; and each nature remained at all times united in the one person of Jesus, the Christ. Jesus did not at any time switch back and forth between the two natures, so that at one moment he is only human and the next moment he is only divine. Would this not have turned Jesus into a schizophrenic? The deity did not become humanity, and the humanity was not transformed into deity. At all times, the two natures remained *united* in the one persons of Jesus Christ so that, at all times, he was both fully human and fully divine. In this way, the Church rejected any idea of

a natural union of the two natures of Christ into some kind of a God/Man who was neither truly human nor truly divine.

This brief summary of the doctrine of the Two Natures of Christ is presented as back story to the earlier conclusion that the divine maternity of Mary serves as a defense of the Two Natures doctrine of Christ. Here the point is that Mary bears the Incarnate God into this world for our salvation. This title *Theotokos* enshrines forever this unique and blessed role the Holy Virgin fulfilled in God's plan on our behalf. Mary, and no other but she alone, was chosen by God to be the holy vessel for God to come among us as a human being. Mary, and no other, will forever in the Church be called the *Theotokos*. While this is a Greek term, I do not think that is an impediment to its use by Protestant Christians. In fact, it may be an advantage. It allows Protestants to make use of a centrally important and even fundamental title for Mary that affirms her divine maternity without the centuries of bias and resistance to the nearly equivalent title Mother of God.

As Protestant Christians learn to appreciate what these two titles for the divine maternity are meant to preserve, namely the doctrine of Christ, they may be enabled both to affirm them and to begin incorporating them into their faith and common worship. It may be helpful for Protestant Christians, who may still be uncomfortable with a title like Mother of God, to begin by using the title Mother of God Incarnate, or Mother of God the Son, or even *Theotokos*. This may be a good place to start when introducing congregations to this unfamiliar title for Mary. An examination of these two titles for Mary suggests Protestant Christians would benefit greatly by further study of the many titles given to the Holy Mother. Pastors may choose to lead an adult study group on the topic of Mary as a way of initiating a recovery of Mary to her rightful place in their congregation's faith and worship. Study questions are included at the end of each chapter of this book, so that this book may be used with adult study groups in the church.

Then may come to past the ecumenical hope that Vatican II expressed concerning Mary, "Joined to Christ the Head, and in communion with all his saints, the faithful must in the first place reverence the memory 'of the glorious ever Virgin Mary, Mother of God and of our Lord Jesus Christ,'…She is hailed as preeminent and as a wholly unique member of the Church, and as its type and outstanding model in faith and charity."[38] Hail Mary, full of grace!

Chapter 10: Study Aids

1. Titles are a significant way theology develops. Vatican II offered this guidance for
titles for the Virgin Mary, "Let them rightly explain the office and privileges of the Blessed Virgin which are always related to Christ, the source of all truth, sanctity, and piety." How does this guidance help Protestant Christians approach Mary?

2. The author writes, "If the reforms of Marian devotion that we have called for as Protestant Christians are now being addressed and even embraced by the Catholic Church, does that not require of us to look again at Mary and her place in the tradition with fresh eyes?" How do you respond to this statement?

3. Citing Tambasco, there are two diverging views of Mary's place with their own theologies: 1) "joined with Christ facing the Church in the work of redemption," and 2) "joined to the Church facing Christ and being redeemed by Christ who is the all-sufficient mediator of salvation." How do these two views help us understand the various titles for Mary?

4. Let's review the list of titles for Mary in the text. (Read the list together.) How do you react to this list, from among the many titles for Mary?

5. With which titles on the list do you have the most problem? (It may be helpful to list on paper or chalk board all the titles that are problematic to group members.)

6. Do you agree the two titles marked with an asterisk perhaps, more than most, have caused confusion and become obstacles in approaching Mary for many Protestant Christians.

7. The author focuses on only two titles for Mary: Mother of God and *Theotokos*. He writes, "They are centrally important titles with a very ancient pedigree; they are not generally well understood among Protestant Christians, and they are often dismissed out of hand." The first title discussed is Mother of God. How do you react to this title? Is it clear what it means?

8. These two titles are basically the same. One is a translation of the other. The title was given teaching authority in the Church at the Council of Ephesus in 431 and reiterated at the Council of Chalcedon in 451. The issue before the Church was the doctrine of the two natures of Christ. Let's review the controversy surrounding the two natures doctrine as summarized by R.C. Johnson (See text.) How helpful is this simple summary of the controversy surrounding the doctrine of the two natures of Christ? Questions or comments?

9. Karl Rahner reminds us the title Mother of God comes out of a defense of the doctrine of the two natures. He says the divine motherhood "really concerns and has more to day about the union of the two natures in the unity of the one person of the Word of God than about Mary herself." How does it help us to appreciate this title once we understand its purpose to defend the doctrine of the two natures of Christ?

9. *Theotokos* is the preferred title for Mary in the Eastern

Orthodox Church. It was the title originally used at Chalcedon and was translated in the West as Mother of God. Let's read together the author's paragraph at the beginning of the discussion of this title. How helpful is this title which means "God bearer?"

10. Vatican II expressed this ecumenical hope concerning Mary, "Joined to Christ the Head, and in communion with al his saints, the faithful must in the first place reverence the memory 'of the glorious ever Virgin Mary, Mother of God, and of our Lord Jesus Christ,'...She is hailed as preeminent and as a wholly unique member of the Church, and as its type and outstanding model in faith and charity." Reactions and responses? Is their any problem with this ecumenical hope?

11. Let us close this session by saying together responsively a call to worship numbered 4, in Part II of this study book.

CHAPTER 11
A WAY FORWARD

Once we have discovered Mary in both the Text and the Tradition, what now shall we do? Can we allow her to take her rightful place in our faith and in our worship? What then is Mary's rightful place? It is apparent this brief journey to discover Mary has raised a number of important questions. A way forward for many of us is still uncertain. I do believe a way forward for us as Protestant Christians means we can no longer be self-satisfied simply to say what we do not believe about Mary. A way forward means we will need to begin focusing on what we can believe about Mary. I know that will be difficult for some. It may even be difficult for many. However, the alternative is to remain locked in a dark room that has been sealed up for more than 500 years! The world has become too small a place for Protestant Christians to be stuck in the past. The family of God is too precious for Christians to continue fighting among ourselves over long forgotten battles.

For now however, we need to ask ourselves how we can continue to ignore Mary and remain faithful to our own

Protestant heritage? We take pride in our mantra: "God alone, grace alone, faith alone, Christ alone, scripture alone." These phrases served as a kind of battle-cry of the Protestant Reformation. Yet, we continue our total silence about Mary. How long can we continue to make Mary a battleground between Catholics and Protestants? Isn't more than 500 years long enough? Granted there are still many outstanding issues about Mariology that are troubling to Protestants. These issues are now being properly addressed in ecumenical dialogue. There are ongoing Lutheran-Catholic dialogue and Anglican-Catholic dialogue. These dialogues hold the promise of increased understanding of the issues regarding Mary for both sides. While these ecumenical discussions about the place and importance of Mary may help Protestants recover an appreciation for Mary, they will take time.

Mary's place among the first followers of Jesus and in the early church is enshrined in scripture. How is it then that when we Protestant Christians encounter Mary in the text for Advent or Christmas, too often the text is subverted away from the subject matter of the text? How often will we continue dodging Mary in the biblical text? We can not continue to do what a pastor colleague of mine once told me he does when Mary appears in the biblical text. He preaches on family life! He does not preach on the subject of the text, which on that Sunday is Mary. How can we avoid talking and preaching about this woman of amazing faithfulness and obedience to God? Why would we? How can we, in faithfulness to our Protestant heritage, pretend she is not there in the text? When Mary appears in the text, she is named thus emphasizing her place of prominence among the followers of Jesus. The way forward certainly will include that we Protestants need to remain faithful to our principle of allowing the biblical text to speak its message without constraint and without preconditions. We subvert the text when we allow our anti-Catholic and anti-Mary biases confine what we allow the text say to us. How long will we continue to avoid Mary in the biblical text? Why would we want to?

I believe there is a way forward for us Protestant Christians to find a place for Mary in our faith and in our worship. Following is a list of small steps that can be taken to begin one's own journey. For those who practice Marion devotion, these small steps may appear insignificant. But, I remind them the Catholic Church did not arrive quickly at its present position of venerating Mary. It took 20 centuries. There were Church Councils, debates, controversies, declarations, Papal Bulls. However, these small steps are a beginning. They begin to map a way forward. We can not continue to remain silent about this amazing woman whose faithfulness and obedience to God is truly a model of Christian discipleship. Here I outline a way to begin our recovery of Mary in our Protestant faith and worship. I have divided the steps into two categories. The first list of steps is for all Protestant Christians both laity and clergy. The second list is specifically for my Protestant colleagues in ordained ministry.

A Way Forward for Protestant Laity and Clergy

This first list of steps in recognizing the place and importance of Mary is intended for both laity and clergy in the Protestant tradition. As you read each step, ask yourself if you can take this step now.

1. *Mary can be affirmed and recognized for what she truly is, a model for all Christians.* Who is not amazed to read the story of the Annunciation when the angel visits Mary to tell her she has been chosen by God to bear God's only begotten Son into the world? This startling and demanding news is met by Mary with perfect faith and obedience. Mary responds to the message of the angel,

"Behold, I am the handmaid of the Lord; let it be to me according to your word." (Luke 1:38a)

2. *Mary can be affirmed and given her proper place in our faith and worship without subscribing to all the Catholic Church's teachings regarding Mary that have accumulated over the centuries.* It is not an either/or choice. We are not asked *either* to believe everything the Catholic Church has taught about Mary *or* remain silent about Mary and ignore her completely. In the past, I believe Protestant Christians have approached the question of Mary in terms of an either/or decision. It is time we moved forward and get beyond the polemic of the past. We Protestants need to focus on what we are *for* rather than only what we are *against*. It is time for us to decide what we can believe about Mary rather than what we can't believe about Mary.

3. *Mary can be recognized for her divine maternity.* She was chosen by God for this special role in God's plan for our salvation. Mary, and no one else, was chosen by God for this divine purpose. She and she alone was God's choice to be the *Theotokos*, the God Bearer or Mother of God incarnate. However, this choosing required Mary's consent. She was asked by God to bear God into human flesh. Mary obediently said 'Yes' to God's heavenly messenger and put her whole self in the saying. This unreserved obedience on the part of Mary suggests her divine maternity was first realized in Mary's spirit before it was realized in her flesh. Or, as St. Augustine stated it, "Mary conceived Jesus in her mind and heart before she conceived him in her womb."[39] This surely merits Mary's recognition and praise by us.

4. *Mary can be recognized in our faith for her rightful place among the earliest believers in Jesus Christ.* Mary knew before anyone else who Jesus was and for what special purpose he was born into the world. She believed in God's promise in Jesus Christ from before his conception, because without her joyful consent she would not

have become the *Theotokos*. It is, therefore, altogether appropriate to consider Mary to be the first disciple because she was the first to believe.

5. *Mary can deepen our devotional life as we look to her as one of the chief of all Mothers in the faith.* While we may not practice a Marian devotion as do our Catholic sisters and brothers, we can begin to allow Mary as our Mother of the Church to coach us in our piety. This does not mean we ask her to mediate between our Lord and us, as though she occupies some special place between Christ and us. It means we recognize that Mary, the Mother of our Lord and one of the first disciples, can help us learn to yield our lives more fully to Christ and open ourselves more fully to the working of the Holy Spirit. In these ways, we are helped to receive more of the life of God into our lives and enabled to live the life of God more fully into the world.

A Way Forward for Protestant Clergy

While the above list of steps in recognizing the place and importance of Mary is intended for both laity and clergy, this second list of steps is specifically meant for my colleagues in ordained ministry. For they are chiefly responsible for leadership in planning worship, and they are among the chief leaders in developing a program of ministries in the local church. As my colleagues read each step, ask yourself if you are able and ready to take this step now.

1. *Mary can be the subject of a biblical text for preaching.* Mary appears not only in the nativity stories of Jesus' birth; she also appears in the ministry of Jesus, at the crucifixion, and in the early church. Whenever Mary appears in the text, she is named, and this naming indicates her prominence among the disciples and among the members of the early church. Her place in the text is secure. We don't have to preach about family life or some other diversion to

avoid Mary in the biblical text. She stands tall among the great saints of the Church.

2. *Mary can be the subject of adult study groups in Protestant Churches.* Where will we find a better example of faithfulness to the call of God upon a human life? Where will we find a better example of how to say 'yes' to God? Where will we find a better example of self-giving obedience to the will of God? A study group on the topic of Mary will allow the laity to work together in their understanding of Mary and her importance in the biblical witness and in the church.

3. *Mary can be the subject of Christian Education studies for children and youth.* Since Mary was a prominent member in the Jerusalem Church as well as the mother of our Lord, she would be an appropriate subject for Christian Education. I have seen units of Christian Education on Paul and other key persons in the life of the early Church. Why not, then, a unit on Mary?

4. *Mary can be the subject of continuing education for clergy.* I suspect there are many clergy who have not kept well informed about the developments regarding Mary during and since Vatican II. The Council, it has been observed, marked a "watershed of a movement in theology toward a new methodology."[40] This change marked a profound renewal of the Catholic Church. This new methodology emphasized the role of biblical studies and revelation in defining and interpreting the theology of the church. No where was this new emphasis on revelation more noticeable than in the Catholic Church's teaching regarding Mary. This new theological emphasis with its stress on the biblical witness was apparent in the Council's statementst on Mary. Tambasco describes the change this way, "The new text started from the sources of revelation, putting heavy emphasis on Scripture and relating Scripture to tradition in a more dynamic and intimate way."[41] Protestant clergy need to catch up with the developments that have been taking place in Marian theology. Unfortunately, Mary has not yet appeared on many

pastors theological radar screens.

5. *Mary can rightfully, be acknowledged in our worship and liturgy.* As an important figure in the N.T., Mary deserves to be recognized in our liturgy as well as in our worship. Appropriate references to Mary both as Mother of our Lord and as one of the earliest disciples may be made both in worship and liturgy. Although such references to Mary will be featured during Advent and Christmas, they need not be limited to those two seasons of the Church year. In part two of this study, there are examples of how to incorporate Mary into our worship.

A Theological Note for Clergy (And Interested Laity)

It may be helpful for clergy to have a brief note on the theological changes that have been taking place in Marian theology and the issues in that debate. There are two theological approaches to understanding the place of Mary. Both approaches are present and competing in the Catholic Church's Marian tradition. They are briefly summarized as follows.

1. Christotypical theology, which is a Mariology from above, relates Mary by analogy to the role of Christ in the work of redemption. Mary is seen as joined with Christ facing the Church in the work of redemption. This approach distances Mary from the Church and from Christians. She is seen next to Christ rather than with the Church among those who have been redeemed by Christ. Mary is distinguished from the rest of creation. It is this approach, which dominated Mariology prior to Vatican II, and it is this approach that Protestants have found so confusing and even offensive. Mary is understood as sharing in a qualified way in the work of Christ for our redemption. It uses titles like Co-Redemptrix and Co-Mediator. It further speaks of Mary as dispensing graces. Protestants have stood strongly against this view for centuries.

2. Ecclesiotypical theology, which is a Mariology from below, relates Mary joined to the Church as one of the redeemed. Mary is seen as joined with the Church facing Christ who alone is the all-sufficient Redeemer and mediator of our salvation. This approach makes a clear distinction between Mary's rightful place in the Church and Christ's saving work. Vatican II deliberately toned down the notion of Mary's co-participation with Christ in the work of redemption. It avoided any new titles for Mary that would distinguish her from the rest of creation. In this approach, Mary is defined by her relationship with the Church rather than her relationship with Christ and his work. Pope Paul VI, in his concern to define Mary more in terms of her relationship with the Church, gave her a new title at the close of the third Council session in 1964. He declared Mary "Mother of the Church." Some would see this title for Mary placing her outside and above the Church. Does this title imply Mary is outside the Church as Mother rather than inside the Church as member? The Pope, in a bold ecumenical gesture, made a number of qualifications to the new title for Mary that was meant to assure that Mary is understood as an integral part of the Church rather than outside the Church

Conclusion

Pastors and teachers in the Church and perhaps laity as well who have an ecumenical perspective will want to inform themselves about the dialogue now going on regarding the place and role of Mary in the Church's faith and worship. They will want to be part of this tipping point in the renewal of the Church. It is an exciting period that bodes well for Protestant-Catholic dialogue. The way forward can be both challenging and rewarding. I encourage you to make these first steps, as mentioned above, as well as other steps towards discovering a place for Mary in our faith and worship.

Chapter 11: Study Aids

1. What is the way forward for us? The author writes, "I do believe a way forward for us
as Protestant Christians means we can no longer be self-satisfied simply to say what we do not believe about Mary. A way forward means we will need to begin focusing on what we can believe about Mary." Do you believe it's time we Protestant Christians begin to focus on what we can believe about Mary?

2. The author asks, "How long can we continue to make Mary a battleground between Catholics and Protestants? Isn't more than 500 years long enough?" What is your answer to his question?

3. Another question the author asks is this. "How can we avoid talking and preaching about this woman of amazing faithfulness and obedience to God?" Why would we want to avoid her?

4. The author declares, "We can not continue to remain silent about this amazing woman whose faithfulness and obedience to God is truly a model of Christian discipleship." Do you agree or not? Why?

5. The author maps out a series of five small steps that Protestant Christians, both laity and clergy, can take in recovering Mary's rightful place in our faith and worship. Let's review these steps and decide whether we think we can take them or not.

1) *"Mary can be affirmed and recognized for what she truly is, a model for all Christians."* What would make Mary a model for Christians?

2) *"Mary can be affirmed and given her proper place in our faith and worship without subscribing to all the Catholic Church's teachings regarding Mary that have accumulated over the centuries."* How difficult would it be to recover Mary in our Protestant tradition without subscribing to all that the Catholic Church teaches about her? Does it help to know that the Eastern (Orthodox) Church gives prominence to Mary without accepting a number of Catholic doctrines concerning Mary (e.g. the Immaculate Conception)?

3.) *"Mary can be recognized for her divine maternity."* What problem, if any, do we have with recognizing Mary's divine maternity?

4) *"Mary can be recognized in our faith for her rightful place among the earliest believers in Jesus Christ."* Agree or disagree?

5) *"Mary can rightfully, be acknowledged in our worship and liturgy."* The author is not asking us to worship Mary but rather to recognize and name her in our worship. In what ways could we do that? (Note Part II gives examples. It may be helpful to recite together one of more of these examples.)

6. There are two theological approaches to understanding the place of Mary. Both approaches are present and competing in the Catholic Church's Marian tradition. Let's review them in the chapter.("Christotypical" and "Ecclesiotypical.") How does this note on the two theological approaches to Mary help us understand the issue about Mary now being discussed and debated in the Catholic Church and in ecumenical dialogue?

7. Vatican II deliberately toned down the notion of Mary's co-participation with Christ in the work of redemption. It avoided

any new titles for Mary that would distinguish her from the rest of creation. Pope Paul VI, in his concern to define Mary more in terms of her relationship with the Church, gave her a new title at the close of the third Council session in 1964. He declared Mary "Mother of the Church. How do you respond to this new title for Mary?

8. In recognition of Mary's prominence in the church, may we say together responsively a call to worship numbered 3, which is found in Part II of this study.

PART II

RECOVERING MARY IN OUR WORSHIP

CHAPTER 12
MARY IN OUR LITURGY

In Part II beginning with this chapter, several examples are given demonstrating ways in which the Mary tradition may be incorporated into our weekly worship. This does not mean Mary should be mentioned or identified in every service of Sunday worship anymore than we would identify Peter or Paul weekly. What it does mean is that from time to time and certainly during Advent, there are opportunities to heighten the congregation's awareness of the place of Mary, the Mother of Jesus, in the Christian tradition. We may accomplish this by referring to her at various places in the service of worship. It may be in the call to worship, in the "sending forth" or commissioning at the close of the service, as well as in the hymns and sermon.

The following examples were written for use in regular Sunday morning services of worship in churches where I have served as pastor. These examples may be used in a variety of ways. They may serve as models for those who plan services of worship or other religious programs. They may be used to compose your own worship materials. They may be rewritten, casting them into ideas and phrases that best reflect your own emphasis and concern. Some of them may be used just as they are written. I would encourage those who prepare services of worship to experiment with these examples. Your own words or a phrase here and there can give it just the touch you want.

These resources are grouped into categories in order to make them more readily usable and useful. Such groupings also demonstrate a variety of ways to handle the Mary tradition to serve the same purpose. In the following examples the following abbreviations were used: 'L' for "Leader" or "Liturgist" and 'P' for "People."

CALLS TO WORSHIP

1.
L: Hail Mary, full of grace, Mother of the Messiah.
P: We bless God for the Virgin Mary, the favored one.
L: Hail Mary, full of grace, Mother of God Incarnate.
P: Chosen by God, visited by the angel Gabriel, we bless Godfor Mary's faithfulness.
L: Hail Mary, full of grace, whose color blue graces our worship center in this Advent season.
P: Praise be to God who raised up the obedient Mary to bearthe holy Christ Child. [or 'bear God into the world]

2.
L: Praise God our Savior, who comes to us in the lowly birth of Mary's Child.
P: "Glory to God in the highest, and on earth peace."
L: God chose Mary, the favored one, for the divine maternity.
P: Hail, Mary, full of grace, the Lord is with thee. Blessed art thou among women, and blessed is the fruit of thy womb, Jesus.

L: May we rediscover Mary, not as the queen of heaven, but as our sister, our teacher, our model, our Mother in the faith.

P: And Mary said, "For behold, henceforth all generations will call me blessed; for he who is mighty has done great things for me, and holy is his name."

3.

L: In this season of Advent, prepare yourselves anew for the coming of God among us in new and unexpected ways.

P: Like the Virgin Mary, Mother of our Lord, we know that God's word to us is not always what we want to hear, or hope to hear, but what God knows we need to hear.

L: Yet God's Word will be for us a life-giving, life-renewing, life-healing word.

P: We await God's coming among us with both apprehension and expectation.

L: May God's coming bring you the quiet assurance of Mary and the gracious heart of Joseph.

P: We bless God for this hope filled Advent season, and we praise God's holy Name.

4.

L: In the holy season of Christmas, when we remember the song of the angels, the visit of the Wise Men, and the little town of Bethlehem, remember it was God's coming to us that makes this season holy for us.

P: We remember the young and innocent Mary, who gave herself fully and obediently to bear God into our world .

L: In this holy season of Christmas, when we share this feast with those we love, remember how costly it was for Mary to embrace the life God had chosen for her.

P: We remember Mary's divine maternity, how she gave

herself both body and soul in devotion to God that she would become the *Theotokos*, the God Bearer.

L: We bless and praise God for Mary and Mary's son, and for her faithfulness to God.

P: Hail Mary full of grace! Blessed is the fruit of thy womb, Jesus. Amen!

SENDINGS FORTH
(OR DISMISSALS)

1.
L: The Holy Child, born of the Virgin Mary, who is forever seeking to be born anew in us and in our world., wanders homeless and rejected as a stranger among the marginalized people of the world.

P: We who have come to know Mary's son, who is also God's Son, go forth to take our place among the world's strangers and witness to Christ's presence there in deeds that heal and free.

2.
L: May the song of the angels and the joy of Mary fill your hearts in this holy season of Christmas.

P: We go forth sharing the faith of Mary, Mother of God Incarnate, who looked to her firstborn Jesus as "God with us."

3.
L: Christ Jesus, who is preparing for us a banquet in that eternal kingdom where we shall all sit down together and feast

with Abraham and Sarah, with Mary and Joseph, with Peter and Paul, and with all the saints, sends us forth to live toward God's promised future.

P: We go with our eyes fixed on Jesus, the pioneer and perfecter of our faith, who will be our host at that heavenly banquet. (All Saints Day)

4.

L: Go forth inspired by the obedience of the Virgin Mary and the gracious and gentle spirit of Joseph to live your life in obedience to God with a gracious and gentle spirit.

P: We go into the daily walk of our Christian life inspired by both Mary and Joseph and the mighty work God accomplished in them because of their faithfulness.

5.

L: You who have been challenged and inspired by Mother Mary, the God Bearer, to find what it means to be blessed and favored by God go now to bear the life of God into the world of your daily lives.

P: We go from this holy place inspired by Mary, who is a model for all Christians, to live the life of God into all the arenas of our lives with grace and faithfulness.

6.

L: Blessed by God, visited by the angel Gabriel, overshadowed by the Holy Spirit, and chosen to be the Mother of God, Mary has modeled for us what it means to yield ourselves to God's purposes. So go now, yielding daily to the great purposes of God in your lives.

P: We go forth to embrace the purposes of God for us and for our world in hope and faithfulness. Amen!

CHAPTER 13
MARY, THE MOTHER OF JESUS

A Christmas Program with Narration and Christmas Carols
By Gary R. Shiplett

Note: This chapter represents another way to lift up the life and faithfulness of the Virgin Mary Mother of God Incarnate. It is very different from the previous chapters in this book. That is because it is a musical program based on Mary. It narrates the nativity story and incorporates Christmas carols to enhance the narrative. Stanzas from the carols were selected because of their specific references to Mary. This program may be used in a wide variety of settings. It may even be incorporated into a service of worship in the season of Christmas. It was originally written for Christmas Eve.

Introduction

No where is Mary, the Mother of Jesus, more visible and more extolled among Protestant Christians than in the Christmas carols we sing. We may have long neglected Mary in our tradition, but we are compelled to come face to face with her in many of our beautiful Christmas carols. But who is she whom the angel

Gabriel called "favored one"? As we sing stanzas from a number of carols that refer to Mary, I want to explore more fully Mary's person and character. In doing this, it is my hope that Mary will be rediscovered by us as a model for all Christians.

Narration

The Bible reports that because of a Roman census, Joseph was required to journey to Bethlehem, his ancestral home. A census allowed the Roman oppressors to tax the captive people of Israel more effectively and more efficiently. By this time Mary was about full term in her pregnancy. We may wonder why Joseph would have taken Mary with him on such a difficult journey. Since the trip from Nazareth to Bethlehem would have taken nearly three days, it would be very hard on Mary, as it would be for any woman near full term with pregnancy. Perhaps it was because Joseph was poor and could not hire an old woman or neighbor to stay with Mary and care for her during his absence. Catholic tradition has suggested Mary's parents were deceased, so she could find no aid from her family. Therefore, Joseph, for whatever reason, took Mary, large with child, on the 70 mile journey from Nazareth in The Galilee to Bethlehem in Judea, about six miles south of Jerusalem.

Bethlehem, that ancient ancestral home of the great King David, where he was first anointed by the old prophet Samuel, lay about six miles south-southwest of Jerusalem. It is perched in the rocky Judean hill country. When folks traveled in those days, their first choice was to stay with relatives; and since the virtue of hospitality ranked high in the ancient Orient, we are puzzled that Joseph and Mary had to seek lodging at the local inn or guest house. If they had hoped to stay with Joseph's relatives, they were turned away. Could it be that his relatives disowned the young couple because of Mary's pregnancy during their betrothal? "Away with you, for you have dishonored our good name. Yes, the news has already reached us here. Poor child! We wish we could help. But you understand. You cannot stay with us. Go to the local inn and take a room." The inn was not a hotel but more of a hostel, a place for caravan travelers with little place for privacy. Yet even there, Joseph and Mary were turned way because the inn was full.

Hymn: *In Bethlehem Neath Starlit Skies* (Stz. 1-2)
Narration

How far away now seemed the blessing of the angel. How far away had become the joy of Mary's Magnificat when she exclaimed, "My soul magnifies the Lord, and my spirit rejoices in God my Savior!" Persons with less faith than Mary and Joseph may have doubted the heavenly messengers, doubted their dreams especially at a time like that. Some would even have cursed heaven for getting them into such a difficult predicament. Now Mary was focused more on the ever recurring pangs of childbirth that shook her young body in the darkness of that smelly stable, as she tried to find a comfortable position on the straw covered dirt floor. Joseph must have run to a nearby dwelling to enlist the aid of a local midwife. Boy how a man can run when he needs that kind of help!

Legend has it that Mary had a painless birth with Jesus. Paintings show Mary immediately kneeling before the Christ child following his birth. Now I ask you, how many women do you know who feel like getting down on their knees immediately after the birth of their child? Case closed! Christmas is the wonderful story about God's birth among us as a newborn child. God became flesh. I do not think it honors God or Mary to strip away that flesh again and pretend that this was not a real birth. At Christmas, we are to contemplate not so much the majesty of Christ, but rather his flesh, not so much his divinity but his humanity. Jesus' birth was a poor and lowly birth, with only a manger for his bed. His was a real birth and surely a painful birth.

Hymn: *Once in Royal David's City* (Stz. 1-2)
Narration

Born in a stable! Bedded in a manger! Not exactly a glorious start in life. Jesus was clearly born among the poor, on the wrong side of town. Like his mother Mary, Jesus may have belonged to what was then called the "Poor Ones." These were not only physically poor, but they included also all those who could not trust in their own strength but had to rely in utter confidence upon God. They included the lowly, the poor, the sick, the downtrodden, the widows and orphans to name only some. Now suppose if you or I were God and chose to be born into this world. We could show how to pull off a truly impressive, royal birth. Let's see. For a mother we could choose a princess, perhaps one of King Herod's daughters or a daughter of the high priest Caiaphas. Surely, the child would be born in Jerusalem, the capital city and not in some dung-heap town like Bethlehem or even Nazareth. Instead of straw for our bed, a bed of inlaid ivory would seem more befitting our arrival. Certainly, the messengers heralding our birth would not be sent to unwashed shepherds but to kings. God chose a different way, the way of the lowest and most despised, a way that must give place to everyone. Thus, God shows no regard for what the world is and has and does. The world, in turn, shows that it does not know or consider what God is and has and does.

Hymn: *There's A Song in the Air* (Stz. 1-2)
Narration

In the midst of all that suffering and loneliness, Mary was full of faith. As difficult as Mary's pregnancy was, with its shame and condemnation, yet Mary believed. As difficult as the birth of her firstborn was, exhausted and homeless, lying in the darkness of that stable cave shared with the beasts, Mary believed. I do not mean that it was easy for her to believe, or easier for Mary than for us. I think not. For Mary had to believe not only the message of the angel that she was chosen by God, but also that her helpless, newborn son was the enfleshment of "the Son of the Most High." It is easy for any mother to feel her child is special. But this? To be special in such a way! Could this be true? "Could I be the mother of the Messiah?" Mary wondered in her heart, "Why me?"

Yes, Mary was chosen in a special way for a very special ministry. Her body would become the "tent" in which God would come to dwell in the flesh among us. Mary was the first tent under which the Absolute lived as though in God's own home. For the first time, the eternal desire of God to live under the tents of humanity was fulfilled in Mary. God had come to live in perfect union with us, to bridge the great chasm between heaven and earth, to establish God's sovereignty over the earth, to establish God's peaceable kingdom.

Hymn: What Child Is This? (All Stz.)

Narration

Was the dream a reality? Mary's son is born, but is he the "Son of the Most High" promised by the angel Gabriel? Lying there on the stable straw, her young body exhausted both from travel and delivery, Mary wondered these things in her heart. The joy of her firstborn brightened her spirit. She offered a simple prayer of thanksgiving for her child. Suddenly there was heard the sound of excited voices approaching. Were they the voices of Roman soldiers, whose presence may be a threat both to her child and to her? No, they were the voices of simple Jewish peasants. There peering into the stable were several shepherds from the nearby fields. With great joy the shepherds asked, if this were the place announced by the angels where the newborn Savior was born. Mary's heart lifted at the words of the shepherds. "This is wonderful news," she thought to herself, "that I am the mother of the child whom the angels call savior."

A PROTESTANT DISCOVERS MARY

Hymn: *Hark, the Herald Angels Sing* (Stz. 1-2)
Narration

It came to pass that Mary indeed was the Mother of the Messiah. She has also been called the "Mother of the Church" and even called the "Mother of God." In a real sense, Mary is the Mother of us all, for all Christians have come to believe as Mary did. The tragic, but moving story is told concerning a sixteen year old girl named Mona, who was put to death during the Iranian persecution of the Baha'is. Mona was arrested for teaching her faith to Baha'i children in what we Christians would call a Sunday school. While in jail, her mother was also arrested and placed in the jail cell with Mona and a group of Baha'i young women. When Mona saw her mother enter her jail cell, she rushed to her mother and embraced her. Then Mona whispered into her mother's ear. "I am pleased to see you, mother, but please do not treat me differently from the rest of the girls here. Pretend not to be my mother. I want you not to be just my mother, but equally the mother of us all." Later Mona was hung to death along with eight other young Baha'i women.

Mary, too, has become in a real sense the Mother of us all. As the first believer in Jesus, who may rightly be called the first disciple, Mother Mary has helped to give birth to such faith in Christ for all of us.

Hymn: *Gentle Mary Laid Her Child* (All Stz.)

(Here add a closing appropriate to your custom and practice.)

Note: This service may be used in a local church only by the purchaser of this book as long as the source and copyright signature are included. Any program bulletin shall include the title of this book and the following signature: Copyright 2009, Gary R. Shiplett, along with the phrase "Used by permission."

CHAPTER 14
BORN IN BETHLEHEM: A PILGRIMAGE

A Christmas Program with Narration and Carols
By Gary R. Shiplett

Note: This program with Christmas carols tells of our Lord's birth in Bethlehem. It does not focus on Mary but rather allows Mary her rightful place in the birth narrative. It could be used as part of a Christmas Eve service of worship or in a variety of settings. I wrote it for a Christmas Eve worship service. If a carol used in this service is not in your hymnal or you prefer another carol, you could change the text in your worship service or Christmas program. You could choose to substitute a carol that is related to the same theme.

Introduction

Christmas along with Easter is one of the chief festivals in the church year. Yet, it is the shortest season of the church year. It is only twelve days long, from Christmas Eve through January 5. It has only one or two Sundays in its observance, yet it celebrates one of the chief doctrines of the Church: *the Incarnation or enfleshment of God.* God became one of us on that first Christmas Eve. God was incarnated in Jesus of Nazareth, the Virgin Mary's son. Mary, the Holy Mother, was the "God-Bearer" who bore into this world of flesh God's only begotten Son from eternity, the second person of the Divine Trinity. Of course, at Christmas time our thoughts are not on such lofty doctrines, even though Charles Wesley could write these words in his magnificent Christmas carol "Hark! The Herald Angels Sing,"

"Veiled in flesh the Godhead see; Hail th' incarnate Deity."

Narration

Simply put, we celebrate the birth of Jesus of Nazareth, born in a small village in the hills of Judea when Herod was king over Israel and Caesar Augustus ruled the Roman Empire. The village was called "the city of David" after Israel's greatest king, for Bethlehem had been the home of David's ancestors since the days of Ruth and Boaz. It was among the rocky hill country around Bethlehem that King David spent his boyhood as a shepherd watching his father's flock. Around the world, Bethlehem has been immortalized, not as the city of David, but for the city of Jesus' birth. In our service of carols, we will focus upon the theme: "Born in Bethlehem." I invite you on this Holy Night to join with me on a pilgrimage to Bethlehem.

Hymn: *O Little Town of Bethlehem* (Stz. 1 & 4)

Narration

"But you, 0 Bethlehem Ephrathah," wrote the prophet Micah, "who are little to be among the clans of Judah, from you shall come forth for me one who is to be ruler in Israel." Like much prophecy, this one had historical meaning at the time it was spoken, but it also had a future meaning yet to be fulfilled. Surely, King David came from Bethlehem to be ruler over Israel. He founded a royal dynasty that lasted nearly 500 years. Future interpreters would tell us that the longed-for Messiah also would come from the house of David and some believed from David's city Bethlehem. So according to very strange circumstances, Jesus, a Galilean who grew up in Nazareth, was born about 70 miles to the south of Nazareth in Bethlehem.

O little town of Bethlehem
How still we see thee lie!
Above thy deep and dreamless sleep
The silent stars go by.
Yet in thy dark streets shineth
The everlasting light;
The hopes and fears of all the years
Are met in thee tonight.

The writer of these words was Phillip Brooks, a young pastor from Philadelphia who had gone on a pilgrimage to the Holy Land in 1865, just after the War Between the States. He traveled the five or six miles from Jerusalem across the Judean hill country by horseback to Bethlehem. Pilgrims still travel to Bethlehem from every nation on earth to pay homage to the birthplace of our Lord Jesus.

Hymn: *In Bethlehem 'Neath Starlit Skies* (Stz. 1, 2)
Narration

We all know the familiar story of how Joseph and Mary were required to journey to Bethlehem. Rome had decreed that all its conquered peoples must be registered in their ancestral cities and towns. Such a census would allow for a more efficient and effective Roman system of taxation. The gospel writer Luke reports,

In those days a decree went out from Caesar Augustus that all the world should be enrolled. This was the first enrollment, when Quirinius was governor of Syria. And all went to he enrolled, each to his own city. And Joseph also went up from Galilee, from the city of Nazareth, to Judea, to the city of David, which is called Bethlehem, because he was of the house and lineage of David, to be enrolled with Mary, his betrothed, who was with child. (Luke 2: 1-5)

Therefore, Joseph and Mary made the long journey down the Jordan Valley to Bethlehem. Poor, lovely, innocent Mary! And she near the time for her child to be born. After a long, hard journey of perhaps three or four days, she and Joseph finally reached Bethlehem. Remember, she was in the final days of her first pregnancy. How frightened she and Joseph must have been when the inn keepers turned them away because there was no vacancy. In desperation, knowing her condition, Joseph must have pleaded for mercy for his young wife Mary. Did they receive mercy from the innkeeper? We do not know whether they were invited to find refuge in the stable out back as popular tradition suggests. They may have needed to search further. We do know they finally found shelter in a crude stable that was no more than a cave with only a gate at its entrance.

Our pilgrimage leads us to a very ancient church; its very low entrance requires each pilgrim to bow the head to enter. This is the oldest church in the Holy Land and perhaps the oldest church in the world. It is built over a grotto that is believed to be the place where Jesus was born. Is it the exact location? We do not know for sure. Perhaps it is! Since before the year 135 in the Common Era this site was already identified as the place of our Lord's birth. In that year, we know that the emperor Hadrian desecrated the site by building a pagan temple over it. That devilish act, however, served to fix the site indelibly for the future. In the beginning of the fourth century, the first Christian emperor Constantine tore down the Roman temple and built a magnificent church over the cave. That church was badly damaged in the year 529 during a

Samaritan revolt against the Turks. It was immediately rebuilt and that church is the one you can visit to this day. The present church was spared destruction in the year 614 when the Persians destroyed all the churches and convents in the Holy Land. It is believed that the Church of the Nativity may have been spared because near its entrance was a mosaic representing the visit of the three wise men in ancient Persian costumes. Seeing their own fellow citizens from Persia depicted on the wall of the church, it is believed, deterred the invaders from vandalizing the church.

The entrance to the church was changed twice, each time lowering it to prevent marauders from entering with their horses. Now each pilgrim must stoop to enter the very low entrance to the church. How appropriate that all pilgrims must bow their heads to enter this holy place where Christ was born. For we come to Bethlehem not as tourists but as Christian pilgrims.

Hymn: ***The First Noel*** (Stz. 1, 2, 4)

Narration

The news of the birth of the Messiah was first made known, not to religious leaders or secular rulers. The news came first to some of the lowliest inhabitants of Bethlehem who were busy with other matters. Shepherds were taking turns keeping the night watch over the sheep, much as King David had done as a boy nearly a thousand years before among those same hills. Only by the time of Jesus' birth, shepherds were generally hired hands and not family members. They were social outcasts. Luke's Gospel reports that it was to these socially outcast shepherds that the heavenly messenger first came. To these poor shepherds, God sent an angel bringing "the first Noel" of a "great joy which will come to *all* the people: for to you is born this day in the city of David, a Savior, who is Christ the Lord." About three miles east of Bethlehem, tradition has fixed the site of the shepherds' field. There our pilgrimage has brought us into a field led by an old Arab Christian who directs us to a cave in the side of a hill. At night, shepherds, we are told, would herd their small flocks into one of the many caves in the area to protect them from prowling animals at night. There before the entrance to the cave we gather with other pilgrims to sing Christmas carols.

"And suddenly there was with the angel a multitude of the heavenly host praising God and saying, "Gloria in excelsis Deo, and on earth peace…"

When the heavenly messengers left them, the shepherds quickly decided to seek out the new born child. What sign had the angel given them? "You shall find a babe wrapped in swaddling cloths and lying in a manger." In a manger? A feed trough for the beasts? Would God's promised Messiah be found in such a humble place with a manger for his bed? The shepherds hastened into Bethlehem, searching the town's stables. There lying in a manger as the angel has said, they found the baby Jesus. Mary and Joseph were amazed at what the shepherds told them about their heavenly visitation.

On our pilgrimage, we enter the stable-cave, which now lies beneath the church by climbing down a wooden ladder into the grotto. The cave is 35 feet long by 10 feet wide. Near a stone manger, we see a silver star fastened to the floor that marks the spot where Christ, it is said, was born. A Latin inscription on the star declares, "Here Christ was born of the Virgin Mary." The cave seems more like a cellar than a cave because the roof has been covered with masonry since the fourth century. We light the candles that we have purchased from the Orthodox priest before descending into the grotto. We hold our burning candles as our little group of pilgrims join in singing the carol:

"Silent night, holy night,
All is calm, all is bright

I recall when good friends, a pastor and his wife, were making plans for their first trip to the Holy Land. They were visiting in our home, and we shared their excitement. Together we talked about the many holy places they would visit on their trip. Our oldest daughter Debbie, who was then in the first grade, was playing nearby and overheard our conversation. You know how children can hear when *they* want to hear! She came over to the place where the four adults were sitting and spoke to me in words like these: "Can you really go see the place where Jesus was born?" I answered, "Yes, that is what are friends are planning." A bit perplexed, she asked, "You mean Jesus was really born on this earth?" We all laughed. However, the questions of our young daughter are not really so foreign from our own questions. Are they? If Jesus had been born in a nearby community, perhaps his historical life would seem more real to us. However, since Bethlehem in Judea in the Palestinian West Bank is so exotic to us, it tends to make Jesus' own life remote and exotic to us also.

Hymn: *O Come, All Ye Faithful*
Narration

Yet, among the Jews in the hills of Judea in a small village called Bethlehem, Jesus was born. Later he moved to Nazareth in the north, a city overlooking the Valley of Jezreel. That fertile valley, now the bread basket of Israel, is a land bridge connecting East and West. From the hills of Nazareth, Jesus as a boy could look down and watch the constant flow of caravans making their way down that valley carrying exotic things from the East. Yes, Bethlehem and the Holy Land seem quite exotic to us. Yet today, that bustling city of about 30,000 inhabitants bears little resemblance to the picture of Bethlehem in our mind's eye. Nearly 2000 years of history have changed even the little town of Bethlehem. However, the sacred sites have generally been preserved, and, as modern pilgrims, we can still visit them and find inspiration there. There in Bethlehem, we can once again hear the "tidings of comfort and joy."

A PROTESTANT DISCOVERS MARY

We ascend from the grotto having been moved by a sense of holy space and holy place. The song of the angels echoes in our hearts;

"Gloria in excelsis Deo."
"Gloria to God in the highest."

Like the shepherds who were doing their daily chores keeping watch over their flocks on the outskirts of Bethlehem only to be interrupted by God's messenger, so we too can become absorbed by the routines of our daily lives. We too it seems, will need to be interrupted in order for us to hear God's messengers call forth new life in us. We, too, can become so preoccupied with our own busy lives, with our own pleasure or pain, that we hear no song, see no star, receive no heavenly message, and forget that God has become one of us.

Bethlehem remains a charming place in our collective memory, one we all would enjoy visiting. However, does its manger cradle a king? Is "the virgin's sweet boy. .the Lord of the earth?" Perhaps if we do not experience the "tumult of joy o'er the wonderful birth" of Jesus, it is because he has become for us only the exotic one and not the Lord of our lives. If we are to find what the shepherds found in the manger of Bethlehem, then we too must come to Bethlehem not as tourists but as pilgrims seeking the Christ Child. Our pilgrimage to Bethlehem is not for olive wood souvenirs but for a Savior. Something wonderful happened on that holy night in Bethlehem. Yet, it will remain only exotic and nothing more until something wonderful happens in our own lives. May that be so for all of us in this Holy season of Christmas.

"Joy to the world, the Lord is come."
Hymn: *Joy to the World*
(After, add a closing appropriate to your custom and practice.)

GARY R. SHIPLETT

Note: This service may be used in a local church only by the purchaser of this book as long as the source and copyright signature are included. Any program bulletin shall include the title of this book and the following signature: Copyright 2009, Gary R. Shiplett, along with the phrase "Used by permission."

Conclusion

Thank you for taking the journey with me into the biblical text and into the Church's Tradition in search of Mother Mary. Did you find her there? She was not hidden from us except by the centuries of bias that clouded our vision. For many Protestants, she has been more invisible than hidden even in the text of Scripture. Many of us have not allowed ourselves to see her in the text. She has functioned as little more than a kind of "furniture" in the text that has been shuffled around unnoticed. When Mary is present in the text, she is often a major player, and yet we have been anesthetized by our lingering prejudices and biases that prevent us from seeing her for who she truly is—an amazing woman, a devoted believer, a chosen Vessel, an obedient servant of God, Mother of our Lord Jesus, our Mother in the faith, a saint of the first order, partner of God who gives flesh to the Incarnate God, the *Theotokos*, the first believer, a prominent presence in the Apostolic Church (Acts 1:14), and a model for all Christians.

Were you at all surprised by how early in the Tradition Mary became prominent? The Church struggled for centuries to understand Mary's unique place in the Tradition. Does that long struggle depreciate her exalted place in the Tradition? I think not. The Church also struggled for centuries to understand the person and work of our Lord Jesus Christ. Likewise, the Church struggled for centuries to understand the Christian experience of God in Jesus' life, death and resurrection, in the sending of the Holy Spirit at Pentecost, and in the coming of God's Kingdom. The full meanings of these spiritual realities do not burst full blown into our consciousness. We have great spiritual experiences in a moment, but we may take a lifetime to understand them, explain them, and allow them to accomplish their full purposes in our lives.

Mary and her place in our Christian faith, in the Tradition, and in our common worship are no exception. It has taken centuries to reach a full appreciation of this most remarkable Mother of the faithful. In that long process, the real Mary may have become nearly invisible even to some of our Catholic sisters and brothers. Mary, for some, became hidden beneath centuries of pious accretions that transformed this most holy sister in the faith into "a queen to end all queens," a static statue robed as a Madonna prominent on Catholic Church altars. The Second Vatican Council has done much to help Christians, both Catholic and Protestant, recover the fullness of Mary's place in the Church's Scripture and Tradition. It opened a door to Protestants who hardly knew Mary and invited them to meet her anew. Likewise the Catholic devout were invited to seek Mary anew beyond all the centuries of pious enthusiasm. The Catholic monk Carlo Carretto, who has taken Mary as his religious teacher and guide, captures well this tipping point in Catholic Marian devotion.

I must admit, however, that my relations with Mary, the

mother of Jesus, were somewhat marred by the romanticism of the type of Marian devotion that was all the rage before the Vatican Council and which gradually became empty of meaning...The exaltation of Mary through the enthusiasm of fanatics (so numerous in the Catholic world) end by emptying our devotion to her of authentic theological content. She is, after all, the mother of God and no need of recommendation to be esteemed. Better not betray the Gospel...As with many other things, we had to start again from the beginning.[42]

Can we Protestant Christians also begin again? Can we set aside almost 500 years of Protestant rebellion against "all things Catholic" and appropriate what is best in the Church's Tradition during the first 1500 years? Can we seek to discover what is best in the Tradition concerning Mary of Nazareth? Can we open our shut up hearts to her grace filled life and her costly obedience to God's summons? Will the Holy Spirit be allowed to clear away all that hinders us from learning from this most remarkable believer Mary, the *Theotokos*, the Mother of God? May God give us the grace to embrace Mary as our sister in the faith, our Mother in the Church, and our model of what it means to say "Yes" to God and to put our whole lives in the saying. Amen!

Endnotes

1. *Lumen Gentium (Light to the Nations)*. *Vatican II's teaching on Mary is primarily set forth in chapter VIII of LG.*
2. *Marialis Cultus (Mother of the Church)*, Paul VI, Nov. 21, 1964.
3. *Redemptoris Mater* in *Mother of the Redeemer*, Vatican Trans., Encyclical Letter of John Paul II, March 25, 1987.
4. Carlo Carretto, *Blessed Are You Who Believed*, p. 2.
5. Carretto, pp.4-5.
6. Martin Luther in *Theotokos: A Theological Encyclopedia of the Blessed Virgin Mary*, p. 227.
7. John Calvin in *Theotokos*, p. 94.
8. *Ibid.*
9. *Ibid.*
10. Ulrich Zwingli, in *Theotokos: A Theological Encyclopedia of the Blessed Virgin Mary*, p. 378.
11. *Ineffabilis Deus* in *Theotokos*, p.179.
12. Pius XII, *Munificentissimus Deus* in *Theotokos*, p. 55.
13. *The Dogmatic Constitution on the Church*, Vatican II, in *The Sacred Memory of Mary*, p. 1.
14. Karl Rahner, *Mary, Mother of the Lord*, p. 61.
15. Rahner, p. 54.
16. Rahner, p. 18.

17. Rahner, p. 61.
18. "Wesley Covenant Service" in *The United Methodist Book of Worship*, p. 291.
19. Raymond Brown, *The Gospel According to John I-XIII*, p. LXXXVI.
20. Walter Brennan, *The Sacred Memory of Mary*. This Gospel analysis makes use of Brennan's analysis, pp. 18-35.
21. Walter Brennan, p. 35.
22. Walter Brennan, p. 48.
23. Irenaeus in *Theotokos*, p. 189.
24. *Ibid.*
25. Chrysostom in *Theotokos*, p. 140.
26. Ambrose in *Theotokos*, p. 140.
27. Vladimir Lossky, *The Mystical Theology of the Eastern Church*, p. 137.
28. Quoted in *Religion and Sexism*, Edited by Rosemary Radford Ruether, p. 120.
29. Anthony J. Tambasco, *What Are They Saying About Mary?* p. 10.
30. Cited in "Mary's Intercession: A Contemporary Reappraisal," *Marian Studies* 32 (1981). Summarized in *What Are They Saying About Mary?* p. 69.
31. *What Are They Saying About Mary? p. 11.*
32. Anthony M. Buono, *The Greatest Marion Titles: Their History, Meaning and Usage*, Chapter 12, "The Mother of God." He presents 24 titles for Mary.
33. 'The Symbol of Chalcedon' in *Readings in Christian Thought*, Edited by Hugh T. Kerr, p. 76.
34. Robert Clyde Johnson, *The Meaning of Christ*, Chapter 4, "The Incarnation."
35. Karl Rahner, *Mary: Mother of the Lord*, p. 61.

36. Karl Rahner, p. 56.
37. *Readings in Christian Thought,* p. 76. The "formula" is an alternate translation of "inconfusedly, unchangeably, indivisibly, inseparably," found in J.N.D. Kelly, *Early Christian Doctrines,* p. 340.
38. *The Dogmatic Constitution on the Church,* Vatican II, No. 52. Quoted in *The Sacred Memory of Mary,* p. 1.
39. Tambasco, *What Are They Saying About Mary,* p. 41.
40. Tambasco, p. 3.
41. Tambasco, p. 9.
42. Carlo Carretto, *Blessed Are You Who Believed,* p. 2.

SCRIPTURE INDEX

Genesis
2:15-23
2:18
3:1-19
3:20
4:1

Exodus
13:1-2

Deuteronomy
28:4

I Samuel
2:1-10

Isaiah
7:14

Micah
5:2

Matthew
1:19
1:20-21
1:24

1:24-25
1:25
12:46-50
13:53-55
13:55-56
19:26-27
27:55-56
27:56

Mark
3:31-32
3;32
3:35
6:1-6
6:3

Luke
1:19-20
Luke (cont.)
1:24
1:25
1:27-28
1:28, 30-31
1:30
1:31
1:32
1:32-33
1:34
1:35
1:37
1:38
1:42
1:43

1:45
1:46-47
1:46-55
1:48
1:51
1:52
1:53
1:54-55
2:1-5
2:6-7
2:7
2:11
2:12
2:13-14
2:15-16
2:29-32
2:34b-35
2:41f
2:41-52
2:43
3:44-54
4:22
4:24
6:3
6:20-22
6:24-26
8:19-20
8:19-21
10:38-42
10:41-42
11:27
Luke (cont.)
11:27-28
13:4-5

22:42

John
1
1:1-18
2:1f
2:1-12
2:2
2:3, 5
2:4
2:5
2-12
3;12
7:3, 5
7:5
9:2
9:3
12:1f
13f
19:26-27

Acts
1:14

Romans
5:12-21

I Corinthians
1:19
7:4
9;5
9:5-18
11:3
11:7

11:8-9
11:11
11:12
11:13
12:12
12:13
14:33-34
14:34

Galatians
1:19
3:26
3:27
3:28
4:7

Ephesians
4:21
4:22
5:21
5:24
5:25
6:1

Colossians
3:18

I Timothy
2:11
2:15

I Peter
3:1

READING LIST

Brennan, Walter. *The Sacred Memory of Mary*. New York: Paulist Press, 1988.

Brown, Raymond E. *The Birth of The Messiah: A Commentary on the Infancy Narratives in Matthew and Luke*. Garden City, N.Y.: Doubleday & Co., Inc., 1979.

Brown, Raymond E. *The Gospel According to John*, 2 Vols. The Anchor Bible. Garden City, N.Y.: Doubleday & Co., Inc., 1966.

Buono, Anthony M. *The Greatest Marion Titles: Their History, Meaning and Usage*. Staten Island, N.Y.: St. Paul's/Alba House, 2008.

Carretto, Carlo. *Blessed Are You Who Believed*. Trans. Barbara Wall. Maryknoll. N.Y.: Orbis Books, 1982.

Carretto, Carlo. *The God Who Comes*. Trans. Rose Mary Hancock. Maryknoll, N.Y.: Orbis Books, 1974.

Encyclical Letter of John Paul II. *Mother of the Redeemer: on the Blessed Virgin Mary in the Life of the Pilgrim Church (Redemptoris Mater).* Boston: Daughters of St. Paul, March 25, 1987.

Johnson, Robert Clyde. *The Meaning of Christ*, in Layman's Theological Library. Philadelphia: The Westminster Press, 1958.

Kelly, J.N.D. *Early Christian Doctrines.* Rev. Ed. San Francisco: Harper & Row, 1976.

Kerr, Hugh T. *Readings in Christian Thought.* Nashville: Abingdon Press, 1966.

Lossky, Vladimir. *The Mystical Theology of the Eastern Church.* Crestwood, N.Y.: St. Vladimir's Seminary Press, 1976. First published in French, 1944 and in English, 1957.

Luther, Martin. *The Martin Luther Christmas Book.* Trans. and arranged by Roland H. Bainton. Philadelphia: Fortress Press, 1948.

O'Carroll, Michael. *Theotokos: A Theological Encyclopedia of the Blessed Virgin Mary.* Wilmington, Del.: Michael Glazier, Inc., 1982.

Rahner, Karl. *Mary: Mother of the Lord.* Wheathampstead Hertfordshire: Anthony Clarke, 1963.

Ruether, Rosemary Radford, Editor. *Religion and Sexism: Images of Women in the Jewish and Christian Tradition.* N.Y.: Simon and Schuster, 1974.

Ruether, Rosemary Radford. *Mary—The Feminine Face of the Church*. Philadelphia: Westminster Press, 1977.

Tambasco, Anthony J. *What Are They Saying About Mary?* New York: Paulist Press, 1984.

The United Methodist Book of Worship. Nashville: The United Methodist Publishing House, 1992.